SO YOU WANT TO BE A LEADER?

CHARACTER AND LEADERSHIP
FUNDAMENTALS FOR
COLLEGE STUDENTS

Earl E. Paul, Ph.D.

FOREWORD

As the founder of the National Society of Leadership and Success, I work with thousands of student and student leaders across hundreds of college each year. Regardless of the geographic region or focus of the educational institution, student leaders face common challenges and raise similar questions.

It is with great pleasure that I introduce *So You Want to be a Leader? Character and Leadership Fundamentals for College Students* by Dr. Earl Paul. Dr. Paul has applied his direct approach in identifying and resolving issues to produce a practical guide that will help you build a solid foundation as a student leader. As you read through this book, you will get useful tips and practical suggestions that can be applied to both your professional and personal lives.

While more experienced student leaders may know some of the information in the book, Dr. Paul presents it in way that is useful to leaders of every level. For those of you at the start of your careers, you will find his book invaluable in preparing you for the future by identifying potential bumps in the road ahead, providing guidance on managing through current and future situations, and empowering you to act. For the more experienced student leaders, you will benefit from being reminded about the fundamental basics of your role, the responsibilities you hold, and the incredible impact you can have on students' lives.

As I read through the book, I was reminded of the continual process leaders go through as we strive to inspire others, influence positive change, and continue on our personal journey of self improvement. I plan on keeping this book within easy reach so I can refer to it for real-world examples and guidance as I move forward.

Best of luck on your individual journeys!

Gary Tuerack

President

The National Society of Leadership and Success

www.leadershipsociety.com

ABOUT THE AUTHOR

Dr. Earl Paul works in student affairs and is an adjunct faculty member at Hillsborough Community College in Tampa, Florida. Along with his college career, he is also a speaker and an author.

Some of his main interests focus on leadership/character, goal setting/motivation, career areas, and effective speeches/presentations, all of which he has done extensive reading and studying in as well as utilizing principles he has applied to his own life. He has written about, developed and taught this information to students, faculty and the general public in a number of publications/conferences/presentations over the years.

As part of his professional growth, Dr. Paul has been involved at the state and national level with professional organizations focusing on student affairs and higher education. In his private life, he has volunteered with a number of civic/community organizations including the American Red Cross, the American Cancer Society, Big Brothers/Big Sisters, and the United Way.

A favorite passion is traveling the world, including hiking in the Himalayas in Nepal, spending two weeks in the Amazon rain forest, fly fishing for salmon in Alaska, extensive traveling around Eastern and Western Europe, biking down the Haleakala Volcano in Hawaii and riding a jet boat in the narrow canyons in New Zealand.

CONTENTS

CONTENTS

CONTENTS

CONTENTS

PREFACE

As a student affair's professional and adjunct professor for many years at Hillsborough Community College, a large multi-campus institution, in Tampa, Florida, I have interacted with thousands of students like you. Part of my job has been advising student clubs, including the Student Government Association. I have also accompanied students on numerous conventions stressing leadership development. While at these conferences, I usually present on a topic linked with character, goal setting/motivation or leadership, areas relevant to students as you transition into adulthood. One presentation I developed entitled *Leadership Tips that You Should Know,* which I presented at my college and at a number of conventions, in addition to writing a three part series of articles on the topic, has been well received by students. I decided to expand the topic into book form, allowing me to cover more material and delve deeper into areas that I could not cover in a one hour seminar or in journal articles restricted in length.

Although I think colleges do a tremendous job of educating you, our undergraduates, on the academic side, I believe that the social, moral dimensions do not get the attention they deserve. Not from a lack of trying. I know that universities and colleges do offer leadership classes; yet, many of you unfortunately do not get enroll in these courses and get little exposure to character concerns and basic leadership competencies that would help "round you out" as you transition into the work world.

To help combat this dilemma, I wanted to fill a niche and transform the leadership seminar into a book addressing basic leadership skills and character qualities students like you can be exposed to in an easy to read format with relevant college examples. My wish is the personal interest I have in the areas of character, leadership, and life skills will be conveyed in this book well enough that you can extract some positive, useful information, which you can apply in your lives.

INTRODUCTION

So you want to be a leader? Why? Have you asked yourself that question? Hopefully when you do, you will have some reasons. Well, are you a leader? Can you develop leadership skills? What is character? Do you need character to be an effective leader? What are some necessary traits that mold a strong character? How are character and leadership related?

The traits a leader embodies have been written about, pondered, and dissected for hundreds of years. Leadership and character are both "right up there" on the "top 40" of human topics. Leadership and character are inextricably linked. Although you may have stellar character and not necessarily be a leader, you cannot expect to be a successful, moral leader without possessing admirable character, if people are going to willingly want to follow you. Character under girds all great moral leaders.

Leaders come in all shapes and sizes, temperaments, ethnicities, educational levels and from all socioeconomic backgrounds;

no one size fits all. History is filled with people who seem to have been born with natural attributes of a leader, but if you look at the multitudes of people past and present in leadership positions, you would find that all of them *learned how to be* leaders. "Leaders are not born, they are made. And they are made just like anything else, through hard work. And that is the price we will have to pay to achieve that goal, or any goal" (Vince Lombardi). Good news for those of us who aspire to be leaders but are not sure if we have the "right stuff." Most of us do.

Successful leaders, as history has repeatedly demonstrated, are not always "nice" people and can use their leadership abilities and charisma in negative ways. Think of leaders who hypnotized people with their charisma and style but who had major character flaws (and apparently mental imbalances), resulting in devastating consequences. Strong, famous leaders like Hitler, Stalin, Pol Pot, and Mao Tse-tung and contemporary, but lesser known leaders like Jim Jones (the Kool-Aid guy), and David Keresh (the Branch Dravidian in Waco), all possessed charisma and leadership abilities; however, unfortunately for those who followed them, the consequences of their possessing many defective character traits cost collectively millions of lives and untold suffering.

People are often times categorized as leaders or followers. However, that view is much too simplistic. The main reason is that different situations call for different types of leaders.

Someone who may not consider herself a leader in one position (e.g., a student club) may find that leadership will come naturally out on the softball field because his or her confidence, knowledge and athletic ability all come together to make him or her a natural for others to follow out on the softball diamond. People behave differently in different settings, and one setting may lend itself to one's strengths more so than another.

Nor does a formula exist showing the only steps which will make you an effective leader. Different situations require people with differing leadership styles, experiences, and skill sets. For instance, Mary Kay, leader of a vast cosmetic empire, would probably not be as effective in the role of British Prime Minister (and vice versa). But that being said, certainly leaders share some commonalities of character and action they have consciously learned and developed in themselves.

In the first section of the book, I cover character traits and attributes that I think everyone, leader or not, needs to be aware of if he/she is going to add momentum to being successful in their lives. Based on research, personal observation and experience, most effective leaders personify many of these characteristics. Each one is in bold-faced type so they can be referenced easily, and you can return and re-read those areas that interest you the most.

In the second section, entitled "Soft Skills," I offer observations, again based on working and teaching college students for many years that cover some societal norms (e.g., punctuality, table manners, thank you notes, etc.) which seem to be declining in our society, but are skills you should possess. What I have found from years of presenting this information to students is they want to hear about these areas because some have had surprisingly little, if any, exposure to them and their importance.

In the final section entitled "Other Stuff," I cover themes your parents may talk to you about, but I'm hoping since I'm not your parent (just a concerned person), that you will consider reading about the subjects I included. Why? Mainly because people my age really were your age once so we have been through many of the same experiences you are facing and we have learned from them. Our perspectives do change (and we really do gain some wisdom from living) as we look back on our lives. Working around college students daily, having them come to me for advice, and interacting with them regularly has shown me that I do have some insights that can be helpful, at least based on feedback.

Therefore, some of the material in these areas will seem "preachy." I admit it. So take what you want, if anything, and leave the rest.

Ultimately, my basic premise in this book is that *leadership is learned for the most part* as the Vince Lombardi quote states above. Understand that leadership is a "process," not something you complete one course in and then you're certified for life. Nor can you expect to learn about leadership through only life experiences. Learning leadership is like learning about any other subject. To be one of the best, you must continue to read in the field, take on leadership responsibilities when you can, watch other leaders in action, get a mentor, listen to CDs on leadership programs, attend seminars, and do whatever you can to enhance your skills. Also, although this book is geared towards college leaders, I believe some valuable insights are offered and can be applied as you continue in your college life as well as when you are graduated and out in the "big, bad world" full-time.

One final point before you begin reading: I am gender sensitive about using the third person he or him as was done in "olden times." However, for sake of writing ease, I do not want to use he/she or him/her each time so as not to offend either gender. Nor do I want to refer to one person in the plural sense utilizing "they." As an English teacher, that always bothers me. So what I am going to do is sometimes use he or him and sometimes use she or her when doing third person references. I will rotate those pronouns in sections and will not be using a pronoun as a gender specific one which I think will fit a particular situation. Randomness will be my "modus operandi."

PART I

LEADERSHIP AND CHARACTER

INTEGRITY

In this age of seemingly any behavior is acceptable as long as the person can rationalize it convincingly, who cares what you do or say, how you act, or how you treat other people? You should. And if leadership is a goal, then you must develop a keen sense of honesty and fairness in your personality. The big kahuna, the granddaddy of them all when speaking of character, is personal integrity. At your age you are already far along this path of possessing personal integrity, somewhere on a scale from low to high, whether you know it or not. These character traits are part of what make you the unique person that you are. If your integrity quotient is on the low end of the scale, your chances of being an effective leader will be torpedoed.

What is integrity? The *Merriam-Webster Dictionary* definition states, "adherence to a code of values: utter sincerity, honesty and candor." Basically your actions follow your words. Maintaining integrity is an active choice. When faced with a situation that is unethical or falls somewhere in the gray areas of life, you will have to decide how you will respond. Responding with integrity will many times not be the easier choice. However, As Confucius so sagely points out, "To see what is right and not do it is cowardice."

I was recently cleaning out some boxes in my office and found an envelope. Inside was $80 and a note that said "deposit for Atlanta trip," apparently from a student who had taken a trip with our group three years ago. How it got there, I don't know. But I looked at that $80, knowing that this could be "found" money. I could have put that in my wallet and nobody except me would have ever known about it, and I would have been $80 ahead. But I knew that money belonged in the college account, so I went to the bursar's office and deposited it. Did I think about keeping the money? Obviously I did or I wouldn't be writing about it. I'm not looking for a pat on the back for taking the right action, but illustrating one of the temptations we will have to overcome if we are to lead our lives with integrity. Temptations of all sorts confront us every day. How we choose to respond is what counts. Integrity is "doing right" when no one else is around.

No one acts with one-hundred percent integrity in every situation, but we certainly can find people who have high standards and seek to live their lives according to those standards. The little voice in your head, your conscience, is generally telling you what is right. Shakespeare's "To thine own self be true," comes to mind. Whether you choose to follow that moral compass will be up to you and will continually shape who you are. Work on maintaining high standards in the little decisions and that will help you tremendously when facing the larger ethical dilemmas.

Lastly, when you're leading others, you should realize that you have accepted a responsibility to do what is in their best interest. Leadership should be humbling in the sense that others have entrusted themselves to your care. Possessing integrity will go far in ensuring that trust in you will not be violated.

> *Motivation is a fire from within. If someone else tries to light that fire under you, chances are it will burn very briefly.*
> —Stephen R. Covey

YOU ARE WHOM YOU ASSOCIATE WITH

Did you ever hear your mother say, "I do not want you hanging around him or that crowd"? Wasn't that a pain? But she knew a basic truth. You become like the people with whom you "hang." That is a fact. Thus, you need to choose your friends wisely. Your mom was "right on" in this case because she was aware of the powerful influence others can exert on us. I was reading an interview focusing on a juvenile detention officer who said that in her many years of experience when a "good" kid hangs out with a "bad" kid, the troublemaker always pulled the good kid down and the well-behaved kid never uplifted the troubled kid. A rotten apple does spoil the whole bunch.

This same principle applies to adults. Psychologists will tell you that if adults are trying to make positive changes in their lives, working to change their behavior and their actions, but they keep their old friends who were helping feed their bad habits, then the changes they are trying to make will fail.

I worked with a student, Suzie, a few years back who got involved with a crowd that majored in partying, which included doing some serious drugs and drinking. At first "Suzie" had a great time, but soon enough the alcohol and drugs, long nights and just hanging out with these students took their toll. Suzie's grades dropped, she started getting depressed and irritable, and she found her motivation to do well in college was going away quickly. When she came to see me, I referred her to a counselor. Ultimately, the counselor told Suzie (as Suzie later relayed to me) that she had to get away from these friends who were "dragging her down." At first Suzie did not agree but later realized that the counselor was right, so she made a clean break from the "party animals." Had she not, I think she would have never finished college.

The flip side of the whole association thing is the good news. If you are hanging out with other people who are positive, are involved in clubs or causes on campus, are motivated to help others, are already exhibiting leadership qualities, are looking to the future, are doing well in college, and are generally exhibiting behavior or characteristics that make them "stand out" from the general student population, then you are in good company. Making friends with people whom you admire, who have similar goals as you do, who can teach you and whom you can depend on, now and maybe after your college life, can be invaluable as you continue your college career, also contributing to your leading a better, more fulfilling life. So choose your friends and associates wisely … for your sake … and to make your mother happy.

Everything is possible; it's just that the impossible things take a little longer to figure out.
—Unknown

BE CAREFUL OF WHAT OTHER PEOPLE SAY

People love to make comments, often not nice ones, about other people. They think their judgment of others is "right on," and their job is to share their astute observations. Gossip and negative comments about others are alive and well on every college campus, involving faculty, staff and students.

The first day I began my new job at my college, I met an out-going guy, "Charlie." He took me aside and told me my immediate boss as well as the campus provost were "bad people/administrators" who would undermine my area and anything I wanted to accomplish. Of course hearing that on my first day was not good news. However, within a few days I understood that Charlie was really the one who had the major problems. The two administrators he had been "bad mouthing" were approachable, friendly and willing to help in any way they could. I found that they, as well as a number of other people around the college, had serious problems with Charlie. If I had taken his comments to heart and let that influence me, I might have begun my relationship with these two administrators in a negative way.

We are complicated human beings involved in complex relationships. All people are a composite of good and bad characteristics. Even when we're not always aware of it, our insecurities, jealousies, fears, dislikes, personality clashes, and prejudices play a major role in how we perceive and relate with others. And when people do not like someone or want to get even with someone, making disparaging remarks is one of the ways to do that. Therefore, as a leader, remember that point when others come to you and tell you whatever "dirt" they can. Be open-minded and make your own determinations.

> *If you don't push yourself to the limit, how do you know where the limit is?*
> —**Unknown**

BE CAREFUL OF WHAT YOU SAY

"I have never been hurt by anything I didn't say" (Calvin Coolidge, 12th president). Wise words. Who of you has never said something that you later regretted? Who of us has not had someone repeat what we said to someone else, causing hard feelings?

A few years ago the SGA president had a senator that he did not get along with, a personality clash for both of them. The president was talking to a group of students after a meeting one day and made some unflattering remarks about this senator. By the next day, because people do like to talk, everyone within the group knew about the remarks. Tempers flared when the two came into contact. Although a fist fight did not occur, the two of them had a strained relationship for the remainder of the year, which was felt by everyone in the group. The president learned from that experience that if you are going to make comments about someone else to others, know that the comments will (almost always) be relayed to that person.

None of us is immune from talking about others. We are made that way. But being made that way does not mean that you cannot control yourself from speaking poorly about someone else. You may have to bite your tongue, but it is your choice. Aren't we all in awe of someone who we hear has never spoken a bad word about anyone?

Realistically, too, are you going to like everyone whom you lead and are they all going to like you? Absolutely not. With so many personalities out there, some people are going to rub you the wrong way and vice versa. But, as a leader you must be very careful about what you say about those who are "under you." A cornerstone of leadership centers on trust, and if others cannot trust you to be discreet and keep your thoughts to yourself about them, that trust will erode quickly.

Success is 1% inspiration and 99% perspiration.

—T. Edison

GET INVOLVED

Chances are if you are reading this book, then you are the type of person who gets involved. If you aspire to be a leader, then getting involved is imperative. The fact, too, that you are involved in college is also a healthy predictor of whether you are the type who will be involved in other areas upon graduation. People who participate in college activities/organizations are predictably the same people who carry that engagement mentality with them after college.

And who notices that? More and more people who are responsible for hiring college students, that's who. A large misconception exists "out there" among college students and parents who think that corporations and recruiters are focusing tremendously on grade point averages as a big determiner of who will or will not be hired. However, that is not true. A main characteristic businesses are looking for in college graduates is not the GPA, but whether or not they were involved in some extra-curricular activities. They want to know that you were involved in more than just coursework, that you participated in clubs, fraternities/sororities, honors organizations, or held some type of leadership position.

A track record of campus involvement serves as a beacon light for those who are looking for student leaders. Think about it. If you were an employer and wanted to hire someone, wouldn't you be more impressed with a student who had experience dealing with others, leading others, sitting on committees, making presentations, writing correspondence, attending conferences, meeting deadlines, and handling budgets? What I just listed are the types of skills you can gain from campus involvement. These in turn are skills you can specify in a resume or talk about in a job interview.

Finally, please do not get all excited and show this book to your parents, using it as the reason you can now coast through your classes oblivious to what grades you make. That's not my point nor does it mean that employers will accept a crummy GPA. And if you want to go to any type of graduate school someday, a low GPA will quickly eliminate your chances.

Dignity does not consist in possessing honors but in deserving them.
—Aristotle

ACKNOWLEDGE PEOPLE AROUND YOU

Do you like it when other people notice when you do something right or "above and beyond" what you are supposed to do? If so, then you're like 99% of other people in the world. Everyone knows that we all have an innate desire to be acknowledged in some way. We all like recognition.

In the job arena, the number one factor that leads to long term job satisfaction and group cohesion is being recognized for contributions and efforts, not money. That ties into the misconception many people have, that money is the prime motivator for people's job satisfaction. As a matter of fact, money comes in at number four. So we are not working just for the money. That is why companies have banquets, militaries give out ribbons and medals, universities award diplomas, and your mommy and daddy encouraged you when you were good.

As a student leader, you are in a unique position of identifying those who are making a contribution. So make sure you acknowledge others who are working hard on a committee, who are putting in extra hours, who are being dependable and following through, and who are making sure that the project is being completed. Make a point of recognizing people whenever and wherever you can. They will love you for it

Also, share whatever credit you, as a leader, may be getting for a job well done. Accolades should be shared among the group. You did not do it alone nor should you accept the praise alone. If you "hog" the credit as the group leader, those whom you are leading will be less motivated in the future to support you.

On the flip side of recognizing people, another situation you will find yourself in will be dealing with someone who has done something that is not so great. A key phrase practiced by many leaders is "praise publicly; criticize privately." If it is your job as the leader to talk to this person, then pick your time and place carefully. Do not "let them have it" in front of others. Find a spot where the two of you can talk privately. And if you are upset, cool down before confronting him so you can stay calm and in control while meeting with him. He will appreciate the fact that you used discretion, as will others who know you might want to talk with them in the future for some reason.

I will prepare and someday
my chance will come.
—**Abraham Lincoln**

VISION

We all hear about having vision when referring to leaders. Everyone knows vision is associated with seeing. But vision in the sense of leadership refers to seeing on a grander scale, of envisioning what could be. "Some men see things as they are and ask why. Others dream things that never were and ask why not." (George Bernard Shaw)

Visionary leaders are able to see the possibilities of what could be, and they relish in conveying that vision to others so they can see it too.

However, not only do they see the picture of what could be, leaders convert that vision into a challenge to others, encouraging their followers, obtaining the best from their followers and galvanizing them around a shared goal. Also, to achieve that goal, many leaders work on seeing an issue from more than one angle. They realize adjustments may have to be made to fulfill their vision.

For example, if you want to sponsor the best, most lavish school dance your college has ever seen, you will need to have in your mind's eye the vision of what you want that event to be. Also, to make your vision more effective, you have to multiply it. What I mean by that is you have to transfer that vision to others so they can see it clearly too. The clearer the picture, the better chance that you and your team will be able to achieve it.

Right now your leadership role may be heading a campus club. Do you have any type of vision for where you want to take the people or that club you are leading? If so, that means you are already the kind of person who is visionary. That's "the well" where you will draw your inspiration and imbue the enthusiasm for what you see into others. If you do not have any specific areas you would like to lead your group, then know that becoming a visionary can be practiced and learned. How? Ask yourself questions like what could we be doing we are not doing? What changes need to take place with my organization or on campus that could be done? What is a need the students have that we could address? Without vision, nothing happens, nothing changes.

Besides considering vision on a grander scale for others, start looking within yourself too. Do not think it is ever too early to consider what you see for your future. What vision do you have for where you want your life to be someday? Visualizing is an effective, powerful tool, according to numerous books on goal setting and motivation (included in the appendix), that can make a huge difference in how your life is lived. Ask yourself some "what" and "where" questions too? Where do I want to be in 10 years/20 years? What kind of career do I want? What kind of hobbies do I want to pursue? How can I give back to others? What places would I like to visit? Where would I most like to live? Do I want to be married and have a family? Ask yourself meaningful questions.

Then begin taking time daily, find a quiet place, and start visualizing those areas you want to see happen in your life. See it in your imagination; fill in the details of what that particular scene will look and feel like when you get there. The subconscious mind will then do all it can to make that visualization a reality in your life. What a powerful means to aid you in achieving your heart's desires.

> *Difficulties are meant to rouse,*
> *not discourage. The human spirit*
> *is to grow by conflict.*
> —**William Channing**

GOAL SETTING

Being able to set goals both personally and when leading others is crucial to leaders. Without goals not much happens.

As discussed in the previous section, vision is a mighty force, but if you have a vision with no goals to get you there, then the vision is meaningless. Goals are the vehicles that take you to the visions that you are seeing in your mind. If you do not have goals, then you and your group will be "floundering around like beached fish."

According to goal setting experts, only about three percent of Americans write down goals for different areas of their lives. But the track record for those with goals and those without are striking. Goals should not be broad and generalized. They must be specific, clear, and time specific. The goal of "having the best homecoming ever" is not a good goal, at least not in the sense of goal setting. Better, specific goals for making your homecoming the best might be 1. Book Chevy Chase as the comedian; 2. Increase float participation by 10 units; 3. Budget another $5000 for fireworks; and 4. Have a banquet with famous alumni on Thursday evening. Now you have laid out detailed plans for what exactly you and your group will be aiming to do differently this year.

Goal setting should be a personal priority for you too. People who are more effective in their work life or personal lives are goal setters. Knowing that goals are going to start driving you towards something, set big goals, ones that will enrich your life and stretch you as a person. What are things you would like to do, have, or be? As I saw it so aptly put once, "Do what you want; you are dead a long time."

Once you decide on what it is that you are wanting to accomplish, you should be asking yourself constantly what can we(I) be doing to get us(me) where we(I) want to go? Keeping momentum is a key to successfully achieving goals. Here is where regular meetings with your group are invaluable in making sure that what needs to be done is getting done. Your responsibility as the leader is to call those meetings and track progress.

If you know little or nothing about the goal setting realm,

then you are going to short change yourself in your lifetime. The concepts behind goal setting really work. As with vision, setting and reaching goals is the major theme of numerous best-selling books. Beginning to read those books NOW will have a profound impact on your life. I have listed a few in the index. One that I would highly recommend as a seminal book to get you started in this area is *The Magic of Thinking Big* by David Schwartz. The book is straightforward and insightful in helping anyone understand the fundamentals of goal setting. Once you begin using the principles and see the results, you will be "sold" on why this area can be instrumental in making your life bigger than you might have imagined.

Challenges are what make life interesting; overcoming them is what makes life meaningful.

—Joshua Marine

TAKE ACTION/INITIATIVE

Another characteristic of a leader is taking action. Leaders are not people who sit back and wait for others to get things done. Leaders see a problem and attack it. Taking action ties in with the vision and goal setting areas. Having a vision and establishing goals are commendable, but having a vision and setting goals with no action is a waste of time.

Leaders know that waiting for the right time, the right circumstances, or for someone else to take the lead means that nothing will happen. If you're always THINKING ABOUT or WISHING something would change or WAITING for the perfect circumstances (because those perfect circumstances will never exist).....forget about it. Nothing in life gets done by just thinking about, waiting or wishing it would get done. *You* must act to make anything happen.

Imagine if the framers of the U.S. constitution who had the magnificent vision for a free republic with rule by the people had just talked about it but had never taken action? Or how about the Wright bothers' vision for flight, Thomas Edison's vision for a electric light bulb, or Sir Alexander Fleming's vision for a antibiotic like penicillin? None of these would have come into fruition without a vision followed by action. Have you ever heard someone say they always wanted to do something, go some place or go after a certain goal? Talk is cheap. Overcoming the inertia and beginning to move towards a goal is what counts. Once you take that first step, the second step becomes easier and so on. I had a vision for this book, but the action began when I sat down at my computer and typed the first word.

Know, too, as you start taking action towards any goal, "bumps in the road" will occur. Generally corrections will be needed just like a space capsule heading to the moon. Constant corrections are being made to the course with the capsule actually flying off course more than on but ultimately the adjustments get it to the target. So when things are not working out exactly as you had hoped, do not get frustrated and give up. Persistence towards your ultimate goal is the key. As Henry Ford stated, "Obstacles are those frightful things you see when you take your eyes off your goal."

A sub-heading under taking action/initiative is *do it now*. A monster in all of our closets is the tendency to procrastinate. For all of us, not doing something, putting it off until another time is always easier than taking action now. As an instructor and an administrator who works daily with students, I have found that procrastination is a stumbling block for many. They kept meaning to study but never could quite get around to it. A little mantra used by many successful, motivated people is "do it now." Just keeping that little phrase in mind when faced with something you do not want to do and then making yourself begin to do it can oftentimes be the key in getting that task done. And the psychological relief of getting it behind you, as opposed to dwelling on the fact that it needs be done, is well worth the effort.

So when you have envisioned what you want and set goals

to get you there, take action whether the time is right or whether you feel like it or not. The *feeling* you are waiting for may never come, so overcome the inertia and get going!

> *Leadership is practiced not so much in words as in attitude and actions.*
> —**Harold Geneen**

CRITICIZING IS ALWAYS EASIER THAN LEADING

An aspect of being a leader is that some people will always find fault with the decisions you make, how you treat people, the way you look, and what you did or did not do. Human nature being the way it is, do not expect anything different.

A main reason people like to criticize leaders is because leaders have to make decisions. Leaders make decisions oftentimes once they have considered as many options as possible. People who do not have all of the facts may not necessarily know why you decided what you decided. Or they may have the same facts as you and still not agree with your decision. All of us can look at the same set of facts and because of our individual filters, come to different conclusions. We are totally exasperated at times wondering how anyone can not see what the only logical decision would be (the one we would have chosen).

Another ultimate truth is some people just like to criticize anybody, any time, any place. Have you ever worked with someone who loves to criticize what everyone else does, especially those in leadership positions? In his eyes, everyone is an idiot, a jerk or lame. Have you also noticed that this particular person oftentimes is not in any kind of leadership role? Why? Because sitting back and criticizing leaders is much easier than actually being the one in the leadership role.

As Theodore Roosevelt summarized, "It is not the critic who counts; not the man who points out how the strong man stumbled, or where the doer of deeds could have done them better. The credit belongs to the man who is actually in the arena, whose face is marred by dust, and sweat and blood; who strives valiantly; who errs and comes short again and again; who knows the great enthusiasms, the great devotions; who spends himself in a worthy cause; who, at the best, knows in the end the triumph of high achievement, and who, at the worst, if he fails, at least fails while daring greatly, so that his place shall never be with those timid souls who know neither victory or defeat."

In the future, if you are going through a tough situation, do not forget to give yourself credit for being willing to be "in the thick of things." Remember, too, that in whatever leadership role you are in, from directing the local bridge club to heading a nation, people will criticize you. Expect it and you will not be as shocked when and if it happens.

> *It's lack of faith that makes people afraid of meeting challenges, and I believe in myself.*
> —**Muhammad Ali**

LOYALTY

Why do we love dogs? Because unconditional love, friendship and loyalty rank high. Certainly a dog's loyalty to his master is known and documented. Have you ever heard of Old Shep? Old Shep is the "forever faithful" sheep dog with a statue honoring him located in Fort Benton, Montana. According to roadsideamerica.com, in the summer of 1936, a sheep herder fell ill and headed to Ft. Benton for treatment. His dog, Shep, came along. When the herder died a few days later, his body was crated up and sent back east to relatives. Shep followed the box to the Fort Benton train depot, and watched nervously as his master was put on board and taken away. No one remembers the name of the herder. But everyone remembers Shep.

Because for the next five and a half years, Shep maintained a vigil at the station, greeting the four trains that arrived each day, waiting for his master to return until he finally died accidentally at the station. That is loyalty.

What is loyalty in a human? Should we have loyalty to others like Shep? Are we even capable of that kind of loyalty? The definition of loyalty is "steadfastness in the face of trouble and difficulty, feelings of allegiance, the act of binding yourself intellectually or emotionally to a course of action or person." Men and women who are in combat together form extremely strong bonds because of the situations they face together, knowing that their lives could depend on the other person. Countless stories of people being loyal to others or a cause, sacrificing themselves before they would betray another are recorded throughout history.

In your own life you may or may not ever be faced with a situation that will put your life on the line as far as loyalty. However, when you are leading others, they must feel that you will take up for them, even when it is not always going to be easy for you; otherwise, their trust in you will be damaged irreparably. Loyalty to your people, though, is not to be practiced to the point of stupidity. If someone is doing something that is obviously wrong and destructive, your job is not to be so loyal as to ignore the facts.

Overall loyalty has to be incorporated in your leadership

make-up. A great truism, too, is that your loyalty to your people will be reflected back in their loyalty to you. One of the greatest compliments any leader can have is a person whom she leads saying, "I would follow that woman anywhere she asked me." Be that kind of person and your leadership ability will multiply exponentially.

> *The gem cannot be polished without friction,*
> *nor man perfected without trials.*
> —**Chinese Proverb**

SELF-DISCIPLINE

A main reason that I have students who do not do well in my classes (or could not accomplish something that they want) is not that they do not have the brain power to do well; the reason is they lack self-discipline. Self-discipline is crucial in life, personally and professionally. Why do many Olympians often perform outstandingly in other arenas besides sports? The answer is they transfer the self-discipline they have learned from grueling years of practice to those new areas. The bottom line is they have learned to make themselves do things that they do not always want to do, the essence of self-discipline.

If you have bicycled long distances then you know some of the pain associated with distance riding. The Tour de France, the annual endurance bicycle race, is one of the most daunting physical challenges for athletes held anywhere. The fact that Lance Armstrong won seven times is incredible. In one of his comments in a recent article (paraphrasing), he stated that many times he would rather have been "sleeping in" or relaxing versus riding his bicycle in the cold and rain. He said he certainly was not always "in the mood" to go out and practice for hours on end. The payoff was the thrill he got from winning the tour which outweighed the pain and hours he disciplined himself to spend on his bicycle.

Thus, the ultimate question you are going to have to ask yourself when going for a big goal is "How much do I want it?" If you are the type of person who cannot **make yourself** do something you do not want to do, then you are in trouble as far as life is concerned. Like Armstrong, waiting until you are in the mood or when you think it is convenient will not cut it. Sacrifice is always part of accomplishing those big goals and the larger the goal, the more you will have to sacrifice. That is one of the laws of the universe. Sacrifice involves expending time and effort, making self-discipline an absolute necessity. Sorry, there is no substitution.

As a professor, I have had women whose husbands left them with small children and no type of monetary support. These same women were determined to get a degree and start a new career. That meant they had to somehow manage to work full-time, raise children, keep a household going and take on college classes. Not all of them make it, but the ones who do decided to withstand extremely trying circumstances for many years to get them where they wanted to be. Basically, if you *really* want something badly enough, you will discipline yourself to go after it. If you do not, you'll usually find reasons (excuses) for not pursuing it. The saying, "weak desires produce weak results" is true.

Self discipline is not for the faint of heart. Those who can make themselves do whatever it takes are stronger in character than those who give up easily. Humankind is filled with people who cannot discipline themselves to do whatever it takes to get what they are seeking. These people are left behind by those who understand that self-discipline is required for effective living. In which category do you belong?

Put all your excuses aside and remember this:
YOU are capable.
—**Zig Ziglar**

LIFELONG LEARNING

An attitude that will serve you well throughout your lifetime is an openness to always growing and learning. Look at everything and everyone around you as a potential learning occurrence, knowing you can gather a great deal of information from multiple sources on a daily basis. None of us at any age "knows it all."

Ugh, you say, after I get out of college, I never want to take another class or read another book. Graduating from college is certainly a milestone, but it does not mean you have reached Nirvana and your knowledge base is complete. Leaders in any field are constantly learning and growing, not only about their chosen fields, but they are usually well versed in a number of areas. All of us have rough edges, many of them, or lack knowledge we need to be more effective human beings.

Imagine a jet airline mechanic not being a lifelong learner? Aircraft maintenance changes constantly. Systems change, engines are reworked, parts are updated and whole new aircraft are introduced. Who of us would like to be flying in a modern jet today if the mechanics working on them had finished school fifteen years earlier and had received no updated training since?

You are no different. No matter what area you choose in life, you should be continuing to learn all that you can about it. If you are closed minded about continuous learning then you are hampering your personal effectiveness as well as not adding to your knowledge base in your chosen profession. A way, too, to become an expert in any field is to always gather information related to it. After a few years, you will be looked at as one of the "go to" people to ask when others want to know more about your area. That is a great position to be in for anyone.

Final point: Besides gaining personal satisfaction from learning themselves, the best leaders are oftentimes the best teachers. A natural part of your leadership style should be teaching others around you, sharing your expertise and know-how. Effective leaders leave a legacy of knowledge and mentoring others whom they have aided.

> *Self pity is an acid which*
> *eats holes in happiness.*
> —**Earl Nightingale**

DELEGATE

Anyone who is a leader HAS to learn to delegate. If you think that delegating to someone else is going to be looked at a sign of weakness or you fear that you would be losing your authority

and control, you are wrong. For those of you Type A personalities out there, I know this is a killer. You think that if you
do not do it yourself (whatever *it* is), it will not get done right,
or if you give it to someone else to do, then your job is to
"bug the hell out of that person" to make sure it is getting
done. Trying to do it all yourself is a big mistake; it may work
on a little project, but as you take on bigger tasks, you will
have to delegate; you will have no choice.

A tremendous asset for anyone in a leadership position is
understanding that she can actually lead a much more motivated team with a better attitude if she delegates. Giving more
people responsibility allows them to learn and grow thus feeling
better about themselves. Basically, delegate and trust people to
follow through on projects until they give you a reason otherwise. Does this trust mean that you do not want updates from
someone who is working on a particular area? Absolutely not!
Make sure that you are updated periodically on what is taking
place. Allowing Bill or Sally to get the job done without your
"butting in" will go far in engendering trust in those you assigned
areas of responsibility. A tremendous benefit, too, is that Bill
and Sally get the experience they need as well as a sense of
accomplishment for getting their tasks completed (remember
how important accomplishment and recognition are).

As part of delegation, when leading a group and assigning
responsibilities, make sure that those tasks are crystal clear.

Reiterate them at the end of the meeting. John, you are picking up all of the drinks and will deliver them to the event by 10 am; Jane and Henry, you are going to contact three radio stations and get the public service announcements on the air; and Mary, you are picking up the guest speaker at the airport at 9:30 a.m. the morning of the event.

Ultimately, the more you delegate, the more you will want to delegate. Why? Because you will find that you can assign other people tasks that will free up time for you to tackle issues that are more pressing than what you have delegated. Delegating multiplies your capacity to get more done. When done effectively, delegating results in a "win-win" for everyone.

> *See things as you would have*
> *them be instead of as they are.*
> —**Robert Collier**

DO WHAT OTHERS DON'T WANT TO DO

Have you ever noticed that the person who is leading an event is often the first one there and the last one to leave? She is making sure that whatever needs to be done gets done and is willing to do whatever is necessary to help.

When George Washington was leading his men on the assault at Yorktown, one of the primary means of battle at that time was digging trench works to allow cannons to bombard the enemy. Guess who was in the trenches swinging a pick along with his men? And what effect do you think that had? As the leader of the entire Continental Army, the General certainly did not have to get down in the trenches and his men would not have expected him to. However, he knew how important those trench works were, and he was willing to "roll up his sleeves" (literally) and help get them dug. Leaders do whatever it takes to get something accomplished, whether they relish the details that get them there or not.

Whether you are the team leader or a team member, people on the team recognize who is doing what. If you are fair, if you pull your share of the load, if you are encouraging to others, if you are friendly, if you give others credit for their hard work, all of this will be meaningful in the long run. Those who work with you will remember your actions and attitude and that will be instrumental in how they view you or how willing or not willing they are to work with you in the future. Your actions and your attitude do speak louder than words.

Don't think, just do.

—**Horace**

STRIVE TO IMPROVE YOURSELF...ALWAYS

People concerned about improvement are always looking for ways to better themselves. They read books or listen to tapes on self-improvement, on leadership, on getting along with others, etc. As with any change, motivation and practice are necessary. Do you see areas concerning character in your life that may need some "tweaking?" The best leaders appreciate their strengths but also can see their weaknesses or limits. Oftentimes we are not even aware that a certain behavior we are or are not doing may be hampering us in some way. If you are not sure, ask others. Ask them to be brutally honest with you. They will tell you if they see something and think you really want to know. Remember, we often think we know how others perceive us when, in essence, our perceptions can be wrong.

Benjamin Franklin was famous for making a list of thirteen qualities he wanted to be a part of his personality, so he wrote them down and practiced daily to change his behavior. He graded his progress and eventually made those new behaviors habits. Like Franklin, you can change your thinking and your behavior, no matter what your age. Do not let the psychological theories that state our personalities are already formed by age five trick you into thinking that change is not possible. Remember, though, these are generally habits you have nurtured and are familiar to you, so changing them will take time and conscious effort. Ask the question: what could make me a better leader and a better person and then start working on those areas. Do not get discouraged and give up, saying "that's how I've always been" or "I can't change." Not true. We are all capable of making changes in our lives and character if we choose to do so. Life is all about choices and changes.

> *Know your goal, make a plan*
> *and pull the trigger.*
> —**Phil McGraw**

MAKE UNPOPULAR DECISIONS AT TIMES

Leadership is not a popularity contest. Maybe being popular helped you get where you are, but the popularity thing will wear off quickly once you have to make some hard decisions. Making decisions when you are in a leadership position is not about building one hundred percent consensus from everyone involved. Once you get past one person – you – the chances of always getting agreement on an issue from everyone drops precipitously. As the old saying goes, "you can never please everyone all of the time."

When you are a leader, you are not striving to be popular; you are striving to make the best decision that you can that will benefit the majority given the circumstances. Decisions, however, should not be made in a vacuum. You should be gathering feedback from your people, doing whatever research you can, and considering what will be most beneficial, at least in your eyes.

One of the gravest decisions made in history involved President Harry Truman — whether or not to drop the atomic bomb on Japan. If you read his biography, you will know the decision was not reached easily. He agonized over the consequences for months. In the end, though, after all of his cabinet, military experts, scientists, and congressmen (who were aware of the top secret project) gave him their feedback, the final decision lay on his shoulders. He received criticism at the time of the atom bomb being dropped and continues to have people in contemporary times "second guess" why he made that decision. But even though he knew the decision would not be popular with everyone, he did what he thought he had to do. As the slogan on his desk read, "The buck stops here."

The chances of you making a decision as monumental as dropping the atom bomb may never arise, but if you are a leader, you will make decisions affecting others. And if your decision has any type of negative impact on anyone, then there will be some upset people...and you *will* hear about it. That is what you signed up for when you took on the leadership mantle. The bottom line is you will make some tough decisions, knowing that some people will be upset with you; expect that to happen.

> *Courage is like a muscle;*
> *it is strengthened by use.*
> —**Ruth Gordon**

MEET DEADLINES

When the United States Postal Service says it is *absolutely, positively* committed to get something delivered to you on time, those are strong words. They are offering a guarantee to meet a specific deadline. And people expect the deadline to be met. A characteristic of a successful leader is that he can meet deadlines. The ability to guide people to reach goals and complete tasks within an expected time period is invaluable. Have you ever been involved in a project that required a number of people performing a number of tasks? All it takes is one person not doing what he was supposed to do when he was supposed to do it and the whole project can be thrown off considerably. Thus, if you promise your committee you will have a homecoming float ready by a certain date, then others are counting on you and your team (especially you as leader) to make sure that the float is ready to roll on the day of the event. You are the person who sets, monitors and enforces the deadline. Excuses will not be acceptable because either the float is ready or it is not.

No matter what industry you may be a part of someday, many will have projects requiring time constraints. Being able to deliver on time and effectively will enhance your reputation and help cement your reputation as a person who can deliver. Cultivating that skill now, reflecting it on a resume or showing that you can "get things done" will add ammunition to your employability or worth as an employee.

Be not afraid of growing slowly,
be afraid only of standing still.
—**Chinese Proverb**

DON'T MAKE EXCUSES

If you have taken on responsibility for being a leader then you are the person ultimately responsible for making sure that whatever project you are heading up will be completed. If it is not, then you become the "bull's eye." Making excuses or blaming others will not "cut it." We have become a society of "excuse-makers." Someone else is always to blame, certainly not us. Our courts are "out of control" now because so many people do not take responsibility for their actions. Instead they either blame someone else (and sue), or they make excuses. Think of the "knee jerk" excuses made today like "I did not know the speed limit"; "That was John's responsibility"; "I'm taking medication and didn't know what I was doing"; "My mother spanked me as a child, so it's her fault" ;"I thought she was using birth control"; "I'm in a minority group"; "I didn't know he would tell you what I said"; "I've been meaning to get to that" or "I forgot."

As a leader and a person of character, you must stop making excuses. Start with your own life first. You have to take one-hundred percent responsibility for your life and the results that you have created. In your personal life you are the one making your own decisions, controlling your own destiny, for the most part at least. Yes, for some of you, your parents still exert strong influence, but you are the one ultimately making numerous choices on a day to day basis that shape your life. If you are honest with yourself, you will admit that nobody is forcing you to do much of anything; you are the one in control. Acknowledging this self-determination and accepting that "the force is not just with you (as Yoda said) but is you" is part of entering adulthood. Unfortunately, some people take the "blame game" with them to their graves, never grasping or accepting their role in their own lives.

When you are in a leadership position, whether fair or not, people expect you to take responsibility when something bad happens. The coach who wins the national football championship one year can "do no wrong." However, the next year when his team loses four games, the fans with the short-term memory loss are calling for his "head on a platter." That unfortunately is human nature. Another factor that will seem unfair at times is when the circumstances that caused the negative consequences were out of your control. You know what really happened but trying to list the reasons can make you look worse because others will see the reasons as excuses. You lose either way.

And when something goes awry, you should not be pointing fingers at people on your team, at least in public. If you do that, any trust that you have created up to that point will disappear rapidly. As a leader, you are "the top dog," so you should accept the blame for everyone which in turn fosters trust from your team. Accepting the blame publicly for your team, however, does not mean later, in private, you should ignore dealing with team members who did not perform as they were expected. That is also part of your leadership role.

Think about excuses that you might be making right now: why you do not exercise, why you cannot possibly quit smoking, why you cannot break up with him/her even though you're in a dead end relationship, why you cannot find time to study, why you cannot do a task you promised others you would do, why you cannot pay some money back to someone, or why you cannot quit playing so many computer games. What is your excuse . . . and what are you going to do about it?

> *A good leader takes a little more than his share of the blame, a little less than his share of the credit.*
> —**Arnold Glasgow**

PASSION

What turns you on? No, not that way! I mean what rings your chimes, what floats your boat, what snaps, crackles and pops in your life, so much so that you really like doing whatever "that" is? If you have some clear answers and you spend time doing those things, then lucky you, you have identified some of your life's passions. Imagine your life if you center on what you do well, what you enjoy doing and what keeps you excited; imagine how much more fulfilling your existence will be.

Passion is a hallmark of leaders. Anyone who has succeeded on a large scale had to have passion for whatever it was they were doing or it would not have happened. Think of Bill Gates, Harriet Tubbs (she saved many slaves via the Underground Railroad), Napoleon, Stephen Jobs, Millard Fuller (the founder of Habitat *for* Humanity), Donald Trump, Madame Curie . . . the list is endless.

Here is an oldie but goodie example of a person following his passion. Harland Sanders (Colonel Sanders of Kentucky Fried Chicken fame) had a passion for fried chicken, *his* fried chicken with *his* secret ingredients. Colonel Sanders decided he wanted to get this recipe out to America. Once he decided that, he did not just pick up the phone and call a person specializing in restaurant franchises and say, "Have I got a deal for you," and the rest is history. No, when he was in his sixties, he had to sell a restaurant he had managed for years and start living off of his social security checks (so he was no spring chicken....ha, ha!). But he felt strongly that he had a great fried chicken recipe (with the 11 secret herbs and spices) he had perfected for years, so he headed out in his car, going from restaurant to restaurant, cooking up his fried chicken for restaurant owners. If their customers liked it, he would do a handshake agreement with the owner, specifying that they would give him 5¢ for each chicken the restaurant sold. His passion paid off, turning his effort into one of the largest fast food chains in the world (I have eaten KFC in China) as well as becoming one of the most recognizable figures in the world.

Passion often brings a single-mindedness of purpose, which can be an awesome trait. The person with passion is focused on what she wants to do and that drives her. Some people find their passion for life earlier on, others find it later (and some unfortunately never do). As Henry David Thoreau stated, "The mass of men lead lives of quiet desperation." A number of reasons exist for humans leading unfulfilling lives or desperate lives, but the main one is that many people never find a life's passion so they live their lives day-to-day without much enthusiasm. Find your passion(s) and incorporate that gusto into your life's work to guarantee that you are not one of the masses whose lives are unfulfilled.

It's okay to fail. If you're not failing,
you're not growing.
—**H. Stanley Judd**

BE ABLE TO KEEP A SECRET

Oftentimes as a leader you will have someone who will come to you and tell you something in confidence because it is affecting them in some way, and they think you should know about it. If you are the kind of person who cannot honor that confidence

49

(unless the other person is telling you something that could harm him or someone else), then you will never be an effective leader. Revealing something someone has told you in confidence can "wipe out" any positive relationship you may have enjoyed with that person up until that point. And if those whom you are leading find out you betrayed someone's trust, your credibility will be gone, probably for good with that group. Even if the person who told you never finds out that you told, those whom you have revealed the secret to will wonder what will happen if they want to tell you something they do not want repeated.

A few years ago at the college, I knew two girl buddies who were inseparable. If you saw one, you saw the other. They had a great time together. That was until one of them told some other people a secret revealed to her by her buddy she had sworn she would not repeat. A lot of hurt feelings ensued. Although they patched things up, the relationship was never the same. I bumped into one of the two recently, asked about her friend, and she said that they had drifted a part and really did not talk any more. That is the power of betraying a secret. So learn to zip it or put it in the vault if someone wants to trust you enough to share confidential information with you.

Just do what you do best.
—Red Auerbach

BE DEPENDABLE

Trying to have a career in any field without having the characteristic of dependability is like trying to drive a car on just the rims.... it is not going to happen, at least not well. If you are one of those people who makes a commitment and does not follow-through (and makes excuse to yourself and others), then you will never be taken seriously as a leader and your personal reputation will suffer. Committing or pledging to do something is the easy part; keeping that commitment is what counts.

If you have committed to do something, then you need to make sure it gets done, especially when other people are depending on you. Make promises or agreements only if you intend to honor them. If you really do not think that you're going to be able to do something or you are just agreeing because you do not want to let someone else down, do not agree to do it. It is that simple. That one little rule will help you and others avoid disappointment.

Last year our SGA was sponsoring a big cookout for the student body. One of the students, "Bill," on the planning committee had promised to get a few hundred plates and plastic ware from Sam's Club and bring them the morning of the event. He was given petty cash. The morning of the cookout everyone involved was scurrying around trying to get

51

details in place. Bill walked up to the registration table, plunked down the petty cash and said, "Sorry, but I have not had time to get to Sam's Club. I have class now so won't be able to go," and walked off. Bad news for the event and for Bill. His lack of follow through meant another student had to zoom out to Sam's Club in her car and buy the plates and plastic ware. Thus, Bill's lack of follow-through upset and inconvenienced a number of people who had planned the cookout. Bill's character in others' eyes took a big hit also.

Back in the "olden days" before written contracts were prevalent, when a person gave his word and shook hands that meant a "done deal." Both parties would follow through on their verbal agreement. When your name comes up, you want to people to say, "If Mary tells you she is going to do something, then she will get it done. You can count on it." That is the reputation you want to foster.

Know, too, other students you are counting on are going to fizzle out on you and sometimes leave you in a lurch. Some people seem to have no conscience about "bailing" at the last minute. Sometimes you will know about it fairly quickly, other times like Bill it happens at the last minute. For this reason, you need to be checking in with people on your committee to make sure that they are doing what they said they would do. People lose interest, they decide there are other more important things they want to do, they think their part is too much work, they become ill, their goldfish dies and they are in mourning, they see their grades are hurting and they need to study more or they take a new part-time job and forget about their committee assignment . . . whatever. The bottom line is that they are not going to complete whatever it is they said they would do. The sooner you find out, the better. That is why keeping up with what is going on is so important. Depending on when they tell you or you find out they are not going to help out is probably in direct proportion to your being the one who will have to come in and "pick up the slack."

Dependability has to rank high on your list of personal characteristics if you want to be a leader. Too many people will feel the effects of your abandoning your commitments. So remember dependability and do not leave home without it.

Courage is not the lack of fear, but the ability to act while facing fear.
—Unknown

DECISION-MAKING

As Mayor Richard Daly stated so succinctly, "Whether you make a right decision or a wrong decision, just make a decision. So many people are paralyzed." If you are leading others, decision-making is part of the territory. If you do not make timely decisions, vacillate or hesitate consistently, then your group will feel "rudderless" because you are not doing your job. Will you always make the right decision? I think we all know the answer to that question. Gather the facts, talk to your people and get feedback and opinions as well as applying some thoughtful consideration. Then make the best decision that you can (listen to that gut feeling too) with what you know at the time.

Understand also that you will not always have the luxury for a lot of deliberation. You will be in a situation that calls for you to be decisive – now! A test of any leader is that he can make decisions under pressure, when everything is not going according to plan and circumstances dictate action. For example a major point in the book *Leadership Lessons of the Navy Seals* centers on discussing as many "what if" scenarios as possible before a mission. That way the thorough pre-planning helps those in the field make faster and better decisions because they anticipated many of the eventualities that could happen. Smart.

You and your group should consider what could go wrong in some major event or program you are planning. But know that at times, you will have to be reactive because you have no choice. You will need to make some decisions "on the spot." People will be expecting you to tell them what to do. If you get the "deer in the headlight look" and freeze, then those looking to you for guidance will lose their faith in you. As a leader you cannot be known as someone who agonizes for long periods over what needs to be done. That is deadly and demoralizing. Learn to make decisions when you have to and deal with the consequences later.

Another point related to this area. You are not exhibiting weakness if you change your mind about decisions that you made initially. By this, I do not mean give up at the first sign of resistance. I mean that sometimes circumstances change, you get new information, or your present plan is not working based on earlier decisions. Do not be so obstinate that you cannot look at what is happening now and adjust your plans and decisions accordingly. Being "mule-headed" is not a great trait to possess in "leadership land."

In summary, as a truly American quote states so succinctly, "Lead, follow or get the hell out of the way!" Decisions are part of that leading. Making the call, right or wrong, will be a necessity, so do what you can now to sharpen your decision-making ability.

> *A leader takes people where they want to go. A great leader takes people where they don't necessarily want to go, but ought to be.*
> **—Rosalyn Carter**

GET A MENTOR

One of the reasons my career has not progressed as well as I would have liked in my career at my college is that I did not do the smart thing: I did not find someone higher up, a mentor, to help guide my career when I first came to the college. Do not make the same mistake. What exactly is a mentor? A mentor is a person who provides his expertise to less experienced individuals in order to help them advance their careers, enhance their education, and build their networks. Based on interviews, a common characteristic of many people who have made it "big" is that they have found a mentor. For example, Arnold Schwarzenegger, who started as an immigrant knowing no English, throughout his career intentionally observed, modeled himself after and sought counsel from those whom he thought would benefit him the most. Has that paid off? Considering he was Mr. Olympia seven times, married into the Kennedy family, became a hugely successful movie actor and now is governor of California, I would say so. Here is a guy that set high goals and sought people out to help him accomplish those goals. He had the foresight to realize that others could aid him in his career and life. Mentors can inspire you, tell you the truth (that you need to hear) and help you solve problems.

While you are in college or when you head out into the work world, find someone who can start offering you advice, helping you avoid pitfalls, someone whom you can bounce ideas off of or who may know people in the field you are thinking of entering. There are plenty of people out there, many of them high up, who would be happy and flattered to have you contact them and ask them to work with you.

Maybe you already have someone in mind. So how do you go about doing this? Look and ask around for someone who is experienced and could offer you guidance. Then explain you are looking for a mentor and ask the person if she would consider that relationship with you. It is that simple. And if that person says no or it does not work out, then ask someone else. Eventually you will find someone. Do that wherever you go, in whatever field you are in. The rewards you receive from the relationship will be well worth your effort.

> *The final test of a leader is that he leaves behind him in other men the conviction and will to carry on.*
> **—Walter Lippman**

SHIFTING GEARS (FLEXIBILITY)

To extend the metaphor, when driving a stick shift, you cannot stay in the same gear at all times; you have to shift up or down depending on the speed and conditions you are in. In other words, your car has to be in different gears based on what is required. Staying in the same gear will not work and certainly will not allow your transmission to maximize its power and gain the best performance. What I mean here is that you and your group may be pursuing a certain course of action; for example, maybe you want to have a college-wide raffle to help raise money for a worthy cause. While you begin to put this together, you find out from a school official that having a raffle on a college campus in your state is against the law. At that point, if you are trying to meet a deadline and need to raise money and the raffle idea is not going to work, then "shift gears" and start seeking ways that will get you where you want to go. What can you do to attack the problem in a different way? Being flexible requires doing the best you can with what you have at the moment. This does not mean that you change your mind every five minutes; that is not good and will drive those below you crazy, but it does mean that you can be flexible when circumstances are proving that the original plan is not working.

Flexibility, too, is crucial when small and sometimes large crises pop up at times. All the pre-planning in the world cannot stop the unanticipated; "bad stuff happens" and that is just the way life is. Your plans did not include rain, so the event is moved inside; you and your group must deal with finding out the band's bus broke down on the interstate, the wooden stage you ordered for the show, especially for flamenco dancers, has carpet glued to the top, or the food you ordered has been sent to another campus (yes, this type of stuff really does occur because it happened to yours truly). So expect the unexpected. Know that you will have to shift gears when unforeseen circumstances arise and deal with them the best you can at the time.

> *Leadership is doing right*
> *when no one else is watching.*
> —George Van Valkenburg

DON'T SELL YOURSELF SHORT

I have a challenge for you. The challenge is to right now decide for the rest of the week that you will not belittle yourself, or you will not be negative in the sense of thinking you are not capable of doing something. Instead, over the next week, when you catch yourself criticizing yourself in some way, substitute a positive statement about yourself instead. The sooner you learn to give yourself credit, the better off you will be. Ultimately, too, realizing that you're more capable than you might be giving yourself credit for can have a profound impact on what type of life you lead. If you think you are a capable, confident person who is destined for success, then you will be much better off than someone who belittles herself and does not hold out much hope for big achievements in life. Our lives become a self-fulfilling prophecy; what we believe about ourselves will manifest itself in our behavior and our personalities.

You have become a leader so you must accept the responsibility that accompanies your position. Also, to be a leader you have to see yourself as a leader. Will you ever have doubts about your leadership skills and why you are where you are? Certainly. Everyone, at time, has self-doubts; that's normal. But don't dwell on those doubts. If you don't see yourself as a leader, nobody else will either. And that, at times, might mean faking it. What? People do it all the time. They may not feel as confident as you think they are, but they are doing their best to act that way (and it can be acting). Nothing wrong with it.

Leaders who are in the midst of a tough situation may be "churning inside" and hoping they are making the right decisions, but they do not want those following to know that they are experiencing doubts themselves, so they "fake it." I guarantee you in the darkest days of WWII when London was being bombed unmercifully by the Germans and invasion seemed imminent, Winston Churchill had his doubts. However, he always managed in his public demeanor to display a confidence and courage that kept his people inspired and their spirits up. It's the concept of "acting as if" that you'll see in psychology or self help books. You act in a certain way even though you may not totally feel that way inside and eventually your subconscious will pick up on those "vibes," and it will become a type of self-fulfilling prophecy. Being able to project this confidence as a leader will help those around you with their own attitudes.

Not selling yourself short means you know that you are a flawed human being like everyone else, but overall you trust that you're also a capable person doing the best that you can to serve effectively in your position. Believing in yourself will imbue you with confidence and that confidence will project to others.

> *The quality of a leader is reflected in the standards they set for themselves.*
> —**Ray Kroc**

CHEATING

"I would prefer even to fall with honor than to win by cheating" Sophocles (Greek philosopher). As evidenced by Sophocles' comment, the Greeks were wrestling with this problem thousands of years ago. Cheating is wrong. Unfortunately, as moral values are eroding in our society, cheating is more pervasive. People are always looking for ways to cheat some one else out of something or to find an easier way to get something that they want without putting forth the effort. The cheating wave is alive and well with our younger citizens.

A 2006 survey of 36,122 U.S. high school students by the Josephson Institute shows:

61% have cheated on an exam in the past year

28% have stolen from a store

23% have stolen form a parent or relative

39% have lied to save money

In the college realm, plagiarism is on an upward curve; college professors are trying to keep up with the websites that offer papers for a fee or are trying to determine what work the student has actually written versus lifting it off the internet. Besides education, for many today in business, sports, politics, and everyday life, the ends do justify the means. Rationalizing any type of behavior, including cheating, to get where one wants, seems okay, even admirable if the person succeeds. Conscience is left out of the picture. People continue to swindle older, retired people out of their savings; they embezzled millions of dollars after Hurricane Katrina, and took advantage of families from 9/11. Enron and WorldCom impacted thousands of employees who lost their life savings and pensions. Of course, we are talking about big scale cheating in the examples given, but the seeds of cheating are usually planted when a person is younger, when she rationalizes and accepts behavior at some point that she knows is wrong.

One student, "Dave," served as treasurer of Phi Theta Kappa, which had a club balance of approximately $1500. Dave came from a family which did not have a lot of money. He received an invitation to go on a trip abroad with other students, which he really wanted to do, but he was broke. However, a few weeks later, just before the deadline, he said he was able to raise the money through some relatives, so he went.

A couple of weeks after he was back, I had two students come into my office and say they had concerns that Dave was acting weird when they were discussing spending some money out of the PTK account. Because I knew these two students well and trusted their judgment, I decided to call the bank which housed the PTK account. The bank faxed me the last three monthly statements with copies of all checks written on the account. Two checks had been made out to Dave and two checks were made out to cash, totaling $900. Of course, this was not good.

After consulting with the college attorney and the state prosecutor's office, I and a couple of other college officials called Dave in for a discussion. He denied any wrong doing but could not account for why he had made the checks out to himself or cash. He did, however, agree to pay the money back and was told if he did not do so, the college would file charges. Sad but true. Yes, he paid the money back over the course of a year, but he left the college shortly after his embezzlement was discovered.

Cheating and integrity are mutually exclusive. What should this mean to you?

If you want to lead others, then self respect has to be part of the equation. As Pearl Bailey stated so wisely, "The first and worst of all frauds is to cheat one's self. All sin is easy after that." If cheating others to get where or what you want is not a problem for you whether in or out of college, then you have a character flaw. Cheating in any form means that you lack integrity. Watch yourself in areas like returning money if you are overpaid at the checkout counter, doing your own work on exams or papers, not putting hours down on a time sheet if you did not work them, repaying money you owe to someone, filing your income tax accurately or any of a number of areas that could involve cheating versus honesty. Stopping yourself on the smaller stuff will help you when faced with larger opportunities to cheat someone, somehow. You'll respect yourself more, people will trust you, and you will add another solid brick in the foundation of integrity you are seeking to build.

> *The foundation of morality is to have done, once and for all with lying.*
> **Thomas H. Huxley**

GOING BACK ON YOUR WORD

If you want a "sure-fired" way to destroy trust in those whom you lead, then go back on your word. Have you ever had anyone make a promise to you then renege on that promise? All of us have. How did that make you feel? Not good I am sure. You experienced anger because the person did not follow through as well as hurt because someone had let you done. Ultimately, too, the trust you had in the other person suffered so the next time she said she would do something, you were probably wary. Being burned does that to all of us.

When making a promise, be very careful to do all that you

can to keep it. A salient example from recent history involved the first President George Bush who promised in his first election bid: "Read my lips: no new taxes." Later, during his term however, he did agree to a tax increase; many Americans felt he had misled them, and they did not forget it at the polls. Some believe that broken promise (certainly exploited by the opposing side) cost him his re-election bid. People have a finely tuned memory when promises are at stake. Even children seem to have "memories like elephants," if a promise someone made to them is unfilled. They will let you know about it very quickly. Therefore, as a leader, your word must be your bond. If not, forget building loyalty and trust in those whom you lead.

There's a hole in the moral ozone and it's getting bigger.
—Michael Josephson

THE "F" WORD

I am going to write about the four letter "F" word that everyone is familiar with, a word with power, a word people do not always like to hear. You all know what word I am talking about . . . FEAR. That *is* the word you were thinking of isn't it?

Fear covers a lot of ground and certainly is a powerful emotion. What are we so afraid of: fear of flying, fear of rejection, fear of snakes, fear of dying, fear of Aunt Millie, fear of exams, fear of fear ... the list is huge. And to lead others and to live your life more abundantly, you will have to face fear, stare it in the face, one on one.

A paramount fear for many is what other people think. Have you ever had a time when you would not do something because you were afraid of how others would perceive you? Of course you have or you are not human. However, leaders are risk takers. Many great accomplishments and numerous examples of leaders going against what others may not have approved of would not have taken place had they been fixated on what everyone would think of them if they did what they thought best. Therefore, when you want to pursue something, the fact that "they" might not approve should not be the deciding factor. A criticism leveled at President Bill Clinton was that he sometimes made decisions based on opinion polls, choosing to side on an issue based on what he thought the majority of Americans wanted. When the opinion polls changed, he changed, causing some to accuse him of "waffling" on his stance. If you are a leader, decisions you make are going to require some intestinal fortitude at times because some people (sometimes the majority of people) are not going to be happy with what you decided.

Another fear that paralyzes many of us no matter our age or experience in life is the FEAR OF FAILURE. To help you get over this fear, I am going to tell you something to help you relax. You ARE going to fail at times; all of us do. People who never fail at anything do not exist. And ones who fail infrequently are living a dull life. People who have had some of the major achievements in life are also the ones who have had some of the biggest failures. Stories abound about people in business who made and lost large fortunes many times over, of inventors who failed for years until they came up with the right combination for their new invention, of scientists who fail repeatedly looking for cures for diseases, and of people who were told they had no talent or appeal and later became famous Hollywood stars. Fear of failure is real. Getting past that fear of failure and deciding to forge ahead is what will set you apart from others who give up as soon as the first pang of fear surfaces. In the next section, I will be discussing the characteristic of courage that can help you face your fears.

What you are afraid to do is a clear indicator of the next thing you need to do.
—**Unknown**

COURAGE

Tied into fear is the courage required to face fears. Courage requires stretching yourself. Facing fears is how you develop courage. Courage is learned behavior, not an inherent trait. But like anything else, to develop a trait or skill, you must work on it. If you are not challenging yourself and doing something occasionally that causes you to face fears, then you are not learning to be courageous. What is it that you fear? Once you decide what some of those fears are, go confront a few of them. Tackle one of your smaller fears and gradually work your way up to some of the larger ones.

A great example I have witnessed of students developing courage has been on our visit to the local YMCA's ropes course as part of bonding and leadership development. Some students immediately are facing their fear of heights. However, I have witnessed students who are terrified make themselves climb up ladders and walk across beams forty feet above the ground (of course wearing safety harnesses, but terrifying for them nevertheless). Their knees are shaking, they are breathing rapidly, their lips are trembling, and the fear in their eyes is very real. Yet, most of them make that walk across the beam. What a great accomplishment, to exercise courage, stare down fear and come out on the other side, having done something that was so frightening.

Confronting and working through fears instills courage in you which ultimately adds to your confidence level. At points in your life, especially when in a leadership position, that courage to persevere when facing obstacles or tough situations will be a tremendous resource to draw from.

> *Courage is being scared to death . . .*
> *and saddling up anyway.*
> —John Wayne

SENSE OF HUMOR

The ability to find humor and be humorous is looked at as actual character trait, one highly valued in individuals. If you are not able to laugh at yourself, at situations, at life, you will be lacking as a leader. People have more confidence in you and are more appreciative when they see that no matter how dire a situation may be, you are able to make light of it on some level. Another great benefit of laughter is fostering a healthier body and mind. The ability to laugh also is associated with being more positive, more optimistic. People who can find humor in most situations generally deal with life's ups and downs more effectively.

The ability to laugh at yourself is important, as well as accepting others making fun of you too. That is why celebrity roasts are so popular. Everybody likes to see a famous person made fun of by satirizing her idiosyncrasies, mannerisms, looks ... whatever.

People who cannot laugh at themselves are generally insecure in their own skins and feel threatened when others make a joke or humorous comment at their expense.

Another advantage of humor is relieving stress. Think of when you have been in tense situations or have seen people involved in tense situations and how a well placed humorous comment can defuse the strained atmosphere. Being able to relive that stressful mood can be advantageous when dealing with others.

A president who possessed a keen sense of humor was Abraham Lincoln. Even in the darkest days of the civil war, when so much was going wrong and he was receiving the blame, he would often begin his cabinet meetings with a humorous story. On one such occasion a cabinet members criticized him for doing so; Lincoln's quick response was that humor was the only thing that kept him sane. After Ronald Reagan was shot in an assassination attempt, taken to the hospital and wheeled into the operating room, his first words to the surgeon were "I hope you're not a Democrat." Imagine being that surgeon and those surgical staff members who were getting ready to operate on the President of the United States; his life lay in their hands, and having him make a quip like that certainly defused some tension and helped everyone deal with the situation just a little bit better.

Learning to be humorous is a skill like any other. So lighten up and learn to enjoy and practice humor and the many benefits associated with it. Your stature as a leader and a person will rise proportionately as well as helping you deal with life's situations more effectively.

> *Don't be afraid your life will end;*
> *be afraid that it will never begin.*
> —**Grace Hansen**

LEAD BY EXAMPLE

When you are a leader, people are watching you. Count on it. As far as setting an example, do your words match your actions? Do you live what you are asking of others? If not, your leadership effectiveness will decrease proportionately. People will not follow someone who is a hypocrite for very long. Thus, if you call meetings and you are consistently late, if you talk about others behind their backs, if you do not follow through on commitments, if you yell at someone whom you lead in front of others, if you are indecisive … the list goes on, then your example is being transmitted loudly and clearly.

Great truth resides in the adage, "actions speak louder than words." You can be an articulate person, saying all of the correct words, but if your words do not match your actions, then you are "wasting your breath." My father was a chain smoker and an alcoholic. When I was a teenager, he lectured me about smoking and drinking, usually when I was driving him to the liquor store because he was too drunk to drive. A cigarette would be dangling from his lips and a glass of whiskey would be in his hand. What kind of example was that?

Examine your own life. Do areas exist which you "preach" to others about but do not adhere to yourself? If these areas exist, you need to either quit talking about that area or change your own behavior. People spot hypocrisy quickly.

It is not fair to ask others what you are unwilling to do yourself.
—**Eleanor Roosevelt**

LEARN FROM MISTAKES
(AND DON'T BE AFRAID TO MAKE THEM)

Have you ever made a mistake? Do you know anyone who has? Of course! That is part of life for all of us. Some people become paralyzed with fear because they are worried about others seeing that they have "screwed up" somehow. If that is true for you, you will have to "get over it!" Becoming fearful because you are so concerned about goofing up will keep you from ever leading others. As a fallible human being, do not be afraid to say any of the following: "I've made a mistake," "I changed my mind," or "I do not know." People can identify with all three.

Last year a student ordered shirts for SGA. The students voted to get light blue shirts; however, when they came in, the boxes were opened and there lay 50 red shirts. The student who placed the order said the shirt maker must have made a mistake. We looked at the order in the file and saw that he put down the wrong order number. He continued to make excuses, stating he did not see how he could have been wrong. As the advisor I took him aside, explaining that having red shirts versus blue was not the end of the world so forget about it. But I wanted him to carry away two lessons from the experience. One, the next time he orders some merchandise, double check his order numbers. Second, but more important, after making a mistake, admit it, do not try to blame someone else, and learn from it.

Remember. No leader is perfect. No leader can see into the future. No leader can avoid making mistakes. Hindsight is always a twenty-twenty proposition. You must be able to make a decision and if it turns out the other course of action would have been better, "that's the breaks." You did the best you could with what you knew at the time. Do not beat yourself up. Take whatever lesson you can from the situation and then go on.

> *Victory belongs to the most persevering.*
> **—Napoleon**

COOL YOUR JETS

Are you constantly angry or at least angry enough of the time that people know you have a short fuse? Do other people and life's circumstances drive you crazy so you really have no choice but to get angry? Wouldn't you agree that anger seems to erupt deep from within without your having any control over it, at least it seems that way? If you are angry a great deal of the time then you are probably making yourself miserable as well as those around you.

All of us get angry for a number of reasons: frustration, misunderstandings, fear, feeling a situation is out of control, disappointments, driving in heavy traffic, forgetting to do something important to name a few. Look at the world around us. With strife seemingly everywhere and anger the core emotion behind strife, no one can dismiss how powerful anger can be. My aim is not to tell you to never get angry; that is unrealistic. Probably the only people who never experience anger are permanently high on medications or lying six feet underground.

Some may think that anger is hidden inside of us, almost like a tangible being, waiting and daring an event or person to set us off. But that is not true. Negative events happen to all of us daily, sometimes more, sometimes less. However, what causes our anger is how we perceive a situation and then what we are telling ourselves about that situation. In other words, in situations we are facing, we have a *choice* to react with anger or not. If you telegraph angry thoughts to your mind, anger will result and vice versa. Every emotion we have is dictated by our thoughts (yes, even love as unromantic as that sounds).

If you do not believe me, try this. The next time you are facing a situation that generally would get you upset, consciously say to yourself, "I am not going to let this get me angry. This really is not so bad. I choose to remain calm and in control." Repeat the thoughts a few times. What you will find is that you will remain more calm, not "losing it" as you might have before. Why? Because you made a conscious choice to redirect your thoughts and your emotions followed what you were thinking.

Have you ever observed those whom you consider leaders, well respected ones? Generally they are approachable as well as even-tempered. Even though they may be "churning and angry inside," they often choose to remain calm and less prone to losing their tempers, especially with their people. My point here is not that leaders never lose their tempers nor am I intimating that anyone who loses his temper is a bad leader, far from it. Too many people who are leaders are passionate, demanding people but overall being someone who is not exploding constantly is going to be easier to approach and follow.

Try not to lose your cool, no matter how difficult circumstances become. Ranting and raving at others in front of those whom you are leading will only decrease their respect for you. Staying calm gives you a mental edge and allows you to rationally face problems. As a leader being angry all of the time or lashing out at people unexpectedly hurts the morale among those whom you are leading. Practice keeping your temper under control; you will be a better leader.

> *Life shrinks or expands in*
> *proportion to one's courage.*
> —**Anais Nin**

PRACTICE POSITIVE THINKING AND POSITIVE EXPECTANCY

Can you imagine being around a leader who sees a challenge and immediately begins telling his team that the obstacle is too big, nothing can be done, or we might as well give up now? What kind of attitude would that be? If you want to be an effective leader, then you have to cultivate positive expectancy and maintain a positive attitude. The tone of the group reflects the leader's attitude.

A great truth about life that everyone learns and the sooner you learn and accept it is that life is not fair and do not expect it to be. Bad things do happen to good people and Murphy's Law (If something can go wrong, it will) is in effect for all of us. Is being positive easy, especially when certain things are not going so well? Absolutely not. But being positive is a choice, just like in the preceding section we learned that anger is a choice. As Abraham Lincoln said, "Most folks are as happy as they make up their minds to be."

As President Lincoln so astutely pointed out long before cognitive psychology, people who are positive are that way because of what they are telling themselves. To help you with building your positive thinking, I want to mention one method that can help you change your attitude. The method is using positive affirmations. Psychologists and motivational experts have been advocating their use for years for anyone wanting to effect change in their mental outlook.

Positive affirmations are statements made repeatedly out loud to yourself, but they can be said silently in your head as well. The purpose is to re-condition your subconscious mind to help you change your outward behavior. We are all a compilation of millions of pieces of feedback from our environments (our parents, siblings, friends, other people, our own self talk, our past and the environment). These millions of bits of information are consciously and sub-consciously entering our brains. What you fill your mind with is what will manifest in your life. Thus, if you are prone to be negative and feed your mind with negative thoughts, expect to have a negative outlook. On the other hand, if you want to a more positive outlook and want to look at yourself as a leader, then consider how repeating the following affirmations to yourself could change your attitude.

I am a confident person, and that confidence shows in
the way I carry myself.

I make sound decisions.

I lead people well and enjoy doing it.

I respect other people and other people respect me.

I listen carefully to what others say to me.

I am motivated to do an outstanding job in everything I do.

(Add affirmations for whatever areas are important to you)

As psychotherapists who advocate cognitive psychology have known for years, what you are telling yourself is critical to how you feel and act. Put these affirmations (or the ones you write for whatever area you want to change) on 3" x 5" cards and carry them around with you during the day. When you have a few minutes, repeatedly say them aloud. Besides carrying mine, I also have note cards by my bedside and say them first thing in the morning and at night just before I go to sleep. The more you say these affirmations, the more your subconscious will hear what you are saying and manifest these qualities in your life. And do not just say them in rote, unemotional fashion. Your subconscious responds to feelings. The most powerful method of all is to combine the affirmations with visualization, closing your eyes and seeing yourself as having the characteristics you are affirming. You can trick your mind into believing that you already possess these attributes, helping you to incorporate them into your personality..

Although an older book, the pioneer psychologist, Dr. David Burns, who initially founded the cognitive psychology movement, wrote *Feeling Good The New Mood Therapy*, an excellent resource to read now when you are younger. Grasping the principles of how our thinking dictates our emotions and attitude will be a wonderful insight to guide you the rest of your life.

> *Reason and judgment*
> *are the qualities of a leader.*
> —Tacitus

COMMUNICATE

People want to know what is going on, what may be affecting them in some way. That is human nature. As a leader, part of your job is to inform people about matters concerning them. Keeping people in the dark is usually not a good idea unless you have a solid reason for doing so. Also, do not assume everyone knows what is happening with a particular situation. The rumor mill is alive and well everywhere, so keeping others informed will help insure the rumors are kept within limits. When some news needs to be relayed, good or bad, do not try to hide the bad; relay that news just as you would the good.

Do not underestimate people and think they cannot handle bad news.

Also, as the leader, keeping in touch with your group members means that you will not be "out of the loop." You will be able to assess how people are doing with assignments, what problems or help they may need, if deadlines are being met and any other details that need attention. By meeting regularly, you will all feel like a part of a cohesive team.

Another area people want to hear about is how they are doing, at least how you perceive they are doing. Do not be a tight-lipped leader who gives little feedback to anyone. Let people know what you are thinking and especially give them that reinforcement for what they are doing right. Also, do not assume that everyone understands that you are happy and everything is going fine; tell them when you see them, in emails, meetings or however you communicate.

A premiere example of excellence in communicating involved Mayor Rudy Giuliani and his handling of the 9/11 crisis. He immediately set up a "ground zero" command center, making sure information was funneled to and from that center. He appeared frequently to the press, updating them and the public about what was unfolding, especially since rumors were swirling around and events unfolded at lightning speed. The scale of communications surrounding 9/11 proved "mind boggling." But Mayor Giuliani knew instinctively that he had to inform people (the world) about the latest circumstances in a calamitous situation. The lesson to learn here is no matter what the scale, you should make sure that in your leadership position you communicate with your team.

> *It is the nature of man to rise to greatness if greatness is expected of him.*
> —**John Steinbeck**

BUILD RELATIONSHIPS

Part of being an effective leader is building relationships with those on your team. By building relationships, I mean that you are taking the time out to get to know those whom you are leading, their names, a special hobby she might have or whatever is important to that team member. If you are already hanging out with these folks the "knowing them" will be easier, but, if not, make an effort to get to know those in the organization or club you are leading.

Another point is that you cannot lead in a vacuum. Learning early on that you do not want to be a loner "at the top" can pay dividends during your lifetime. Those who lead by themselves are not as effective as those who lead, surrounded by and gaining valuable insight from those who comprise the group they are leading.

Although the group you work with now might be relatively small, another area that you can start practicing is "management by walking around." A whole management theory centers on this concept. Simply put, as a leader, you are spending time "out and about" talking with people, seeing how they are doing or if they need anything to help them with their task, and letting everyone know you want to be there for them. Do not, however, mistake this for micromanagement. Your purpose of walking around is not to go out and tell everyone how to do their job or give the impression that you do not trust them enough to do what they are assigned to do. You want to be visible and accessible so you are sending the positive message that you are actively involved in whatever is going on.

A president of Student Government a couple of years back was a cerebral type (which is fine), but he did not spend time with many of the officers and senators in SGA except for meetings. Thus his relationship building quotient would have been rated "low." For example, when we went to a large convention, he left the group to go out and push his own agenda. He did this to the exclusion of the students from our college whom he was supposed to be leading. They, of course, felt slighted and somewhat "rudderless." Choosing not to have meals with his delegation further alienated them. The message he sent, the wrong one, said to the group, "you are not important enough for me to spend time with."

An excellent, classic book to read about building relationships is Dale Carnegie's *How to Win Friends and Influence People*. Although dated somewhat, the principles themselves ring just as true today as they did back in 1936 when the book came out (a revision was done in 1981). Carnegie discusses a number of areas that can help you in your relationships with others. The book, as some people erroneously believe, is not about manipulating others for your own gain. Great insights about getting along with others (in a non-selfish way) are covered. That is one of the reasons the book continues to sell so well. So, if you are serious about areas that will help you relate better to others, check out Carnegie's book.

> *Do the hard jobs first. The easy ones will take care of themselves.*
> —**Dale Carnegie**

PART TWO

SOFT SKILLS

SOFT SKILLS

This section on "soft skills" has arisen from my observations of and interactions with students as well as feedback from other college faculty, club advisors, and staff who suggested student areas they, too, think should be included. What are soft skills? I found a more formal definition on the web which follows: "A set of skills that influence how we interact with each other. It includes such abilities as effective communication, creativity, analytical thinking, diplomacy, flexibility, change-readiness, and problem solving, leadership, team building, and listening skills. The goal of soft skills training is to give students the opportunity to learn and practice new patterns of behavior and in so doing to enhance human relations."

Soft skills, just as character development, should be fundamental to all of us. Having basic knowledge in these areas will make a difference in how others perceive you. As you read these sections, decide if you need to address some of these societal expectations. If so, the sooner you start, the better.

SHAKING HANDS CORRECTLY
CAN MAKE OR BREAK YOU

Some people in our society still don't know the importance of a firm handshake. Whether shaking hands means anything about your character deep down or not, the fact is when you give a "limp" handshake, many people notice and perceive a "limp" handshake as a reflection of a negative personal characteristic.

I had a male student relay to me once that he had applied for a job at a company in which he had a lot of interest. He made it through the human resource interview and then was sent to meet the department manager. He went in and shook hands to introduce himself At that point the manager looked at him and said, "I'm sorry, but we really don't have any need to go any further in this interview." Of course the student was stunned. The department head continued, "The first characteristic of anyone I hire is that they give me a firm handshake. If it is limp like yours was, I lose my interest in hiring him. Thanks for your time." That was it. Too harsh? Maybe, but the hard truth is that it illustrates how important a handshake can be to someone.

Both men and women should give a firm handshake when meeting another individual. Combine that with looking the

SO YOU WANT TO BE A LEADER?

other person in the eye; averting your eyes while shaking hands immediately signals a lack of confidence. Men: do not crush someone else's hand (men's or women's) and bring them to their knees just to prove how macho you are. Women: make sure your grasp is firm with members of both sexes.

> *An army of sheep led by a lion would defeat an army of lions led by a sheep.*
> —**Arab Proverb**

LEARN TO BE AN EFFECTIVE PUBLIC SPEAKER

Here's the deal . . . the more responsibility you assume at the college level in a club, or the higher you go up the ladder at almost any place where you work, the better chance you will have of having to do public speaking. For those who are not bothered by public speaking, that is no big deal. But for those of you who need to run out and get a Depends Diaper just thinking about speaking in front of a group, know the fear it generates. I once heard Jerry Seinfeld joking about the fact that most of us fear public speaking more than death. He followed with the observation that if that is true then most of us attending a funeral would prefer to be in the casket rather than delivering the eulogy.

I have a friend with a Master's in Social Work who was recently offered a position of district manager, accompanied by a substantial pay raise. However, she turned it down. When I asked why, she explained that she "hates getting up in front of groups and this promotion would have meant doing that," so that was the deciding factor for her.

Being able to speak in front of others is a skill integral to your success and development. The sooner you accept that fact, the better off you will be. Take heart, though, the fear of speaking in front of groups can be and has been conquered by countless people; like any other skill you have to practice by "doing." Instead of "running the other way," accept those offers that will allow you to speak in front of others. Remember these two points: first, the more prepared you are the more comfortable you will be; second, the hardest part of public speaking is the anticipation. Once you are in front of the group, you mind switches from the "task" of making you afraid to the "task" of actually doing the speech. Your brain cannot concentrate on two major tasks at once, so much of the fear will dissipate once "you are up there."

Lastly, you may be too busy now, but someday when you have more time, join Toastmasters (www.toastmasters.org). This is an international organization that is dedicated to one goal — making the "average" person a better speaker and presenter. Many professionals (including the author) who have had this fear of public speaking or who want to be more effective when they are presenting join this group and experience vast improvement in both areas.

> *A life spent making mistakes is not*
> *only more honorable but more useful*
> *than a life spent doing nothing.*
> **—George Bernard Shaw**

WRITE HANDWRITTEN NOTES

With the whole realm of manners slowly "going away" in our society, if you practice this, you will be light years ahead of the average person. Get some attractive note cards and start using them when you have a friend, co-worker, boss, or associate who has a reason to celebrate, helps you in some substantive way, who suffers a loss or who gives you a gift. Acknowledging that person with a sincere, *handwritten* note will be a special gesture.

President George H. W. Bush (senior) in an interview stated that one reason he became President was over the years he had hand-written thousands of notes to people whom he had met in various jobs he had held. He continued this habit as vice-president and when the time came to put his campaign together for the presidential campaign, he drew support from many of those people whom he had written over the years. That is a powerful way to build a network.

I have written notes of encouragement or thanks to people who have reminded me years later that they still have that note in their desk and really appreciated my thinking of them. Understand, though, that this is not just a manipulative gesture to get people to like you for your own gain, but to let them know of your sincere interest in them. So get some cards and start writing.

You can't measure the heart of a champion.
—**Unknown**

LEARN TABLE MANNERS

Many of you may have decent table manners, but I can tell you from experience that I see many students who are "scary" at a dinner table. For instance, recently, at a large student conference I attended, one of my students did not know how to cut roast beef correctly, so he decided to just pick up the meat (covered with gravy) from his plate and rip it apart with his fingers (no joke). Another student had his face almost buried in his plate, shoveling his food into his mouth without, it seemed, coming up for air.

Although table manners may not seem important now, someday making "etiquette faux pas" at a meal could not only be embarrassing but hurt your career or that first big impression you want to make with the newest Mr. or Ms. Right (or the parents). Knowing basics like waiting for everyone to be served before you begin eating, which fork to use when, what a bread plate is for; how to cut meat correctly, or what to do with that piece of gristle in your mouth, is important and should be part of your basic "life" knowledge. Do not wait until you are in a social situation, wishing you had taken the time to gain the knowledge you need. GOOGLE table manners; plenty of articles exist about the topic.

> *A big man is one who makes us feel bigger when we are with him.*
> —John Maxwell

REMEMBER NAMES

Do you like it when people remember your name? Of course you do; we all do. A secret that many leaders have practiced is remembering names of those whom they are leading. Impossible you say? I forget people's names five seconds after I hear them.

How can you do it? When first meeting someone, make sure that you hear the name and concentrate on it. We oftentimes forget something because we are not paying attention in the first place. According to experts, names enter our short-term memory and usually stay less than a minute. If we are to remember anything, we must first hear it, repeat it (in our head to ourselves), and use it. If you have ever noticed someone you have just met repeating your name during the course of the conversation you are having, he is making a conscious effort to imprint your name and face on his brain. That is one of the techniques people use to remember names. The repetition is conscious, helpful and effective.

Also, in this multicultural society with many unusual names, if you do not understand the way a name is pronounced, do not be shy, ask the person to repeat it; I even ask them to spell it if I cannot quite get the pronunciation. They will appreciate your effort to get the pronunciation right.

And do not lie to yourself with the excuse that you can *never* remember names. That is not true. If you meet a really "hot" guy or girl a party that you would like to get to know better, much better, do you make it a point to remember his or her name when you meet them? You bet you do. Apply some of that same enthusiasm to others. Remember: people's own names are one of the sweetest sounds they hear, so work on remembering names and add that to your social skills repertoire.

A real leader faces the music,
even when he doesn't like the tune.
—Unknown

RETURN PHONE CALLS
AND EMAILS PROMPTLY

I am not writing about returning calls or emails to cable, long distance, or credit card companies who would forfeit their mothers' souls to sell you a product. I am, of course, talking about getting back to people that you do business with or have some type of relationship with in some way. The societal rule of thumb dictates 24 hours (or less) is the magical number, at least that is what was hammered into me when I took sales training with a large company. I always try to make it less. Not returning messages in a timely manner tells the person that either you think you are too important or they are not that important.

Think about how you feel when the person has not returned a call (or email) so you try again, reaching the person this time and she says, "Oh hello. I've been meaning to return your call" (and it's three days later), letting you know that she did get your message, but she has not taken the time to get back to you. The message being conveyed (whether she means to convey it or not) is you are not high enough on my priority list, so I did not bother to call you back. With our fragile egos, none of us likes to hear that. Also with circumstances changing in life as they do, bringing ironic twists, the same person who did not return your call may need you for something some day and could regret slighting you. Wise people higher up the ladder in leadership positions practice this 24 hour rule. So should you.

Only those who do nothing make no mistakes.
—Unknown

LISTENING

A characteristic of a successful leader is a person who (truly) listens to others. Many of us think that we are listening to others when, in essence, we really are not. Listening is a skill that you develop and just like any other skill, you must practice. Entire courses center on listening skills because so many people do not really listen effectively. But the payoff can be huge. If you can listen to someone else, they will "feel it" and respond to that. You are actually paying them a compliment, acknowledging their importance as an individual and that what they are saying is important. As a listener, depending on the size of the group you lead, one of the primary roles you will have is having people come to see you about themselves or others. There may be no action you can take, but the fact that you are listening is important to them.

Another part of listening may be that you will find that you are acting as a mediator at times. You may find members in your group at odds with one another, and your job will be to help them find common ground and work on moving them towards solutions that will be acceptable (for the most part) for everyone. That kind of listening and mediating comes with experience but will be integral to your effectiveness as a leader.

Listening also means asking questions of the person who

you are speaking with, probing to make sure that you are getting what he or she is trying to tell you. Everybody is not always going to agree with what you want to do. This is when you need to be able to listen with an open mind and see if the person who disagrees with you has some valid points. If you listen to her and still do not agree and make a decision the way you think it should be, so be it. But at least you will have given her a chance to air her ideas and concerns.

Anything unattempted remains impossible.
—Unknown

USE A NOTEPAD AND WRITE DOWN YOUR "THINGS TO DO"

No matter what your age or how great you think your memory is, none of us who are multi-tasking can remember in our heads all that we have to do. If you are a busy student with a lot happening both in and out of classes, you will be working on multiple projects at once. With all of the details of what needs to be done swirling around your head, if you do not write the details down, many of them will escape you. At times forgetting to do something you did not write down can be bad news and can cause you embarrassment or trouble if what you forgot was important to someone else or you.

One requirement I have for my staff (including student assistants) is when they come into my office for a meeting, everyone must have a "yellow pad" to write notes about who is supposed to do what. At first, I hear grumbling, but after they see that writing down tasks and reminders do help, the grumbling stops.

So get a notepad, and begin to write down "things to do," constantly reviewing your notes to make sure they are getting done, and then place a check by them when completed. An added bonus for those anal retentive people out there, just checking these tasks off your list will be an extra thrill.

> *Think little goals and expect little achievements. Think big goals and win big success.*
> **—David Schwartz**

USE A CALENDAR

The importance of using a calendar dovetails nicely with the notepad area. Again, the busier you are the more commitments you will have. I see a number of students who have no calendar – paper or electronic – that they carry with them and use. Big mistake. You WILL NOT remember all of the dates/times/places/tests that you think you can remember in your head.

As a professor, I have students who forget that a test is taking place in my class, or they are supposed to turn in a paper or we are going on a field trip on a particular day. In student meetings, I see students agree to help at an event that will take place three weeks away. They write nothing down. It may seem "fresh in their heads now," but many are not going to remember that a specific event will take place at 2pm on October 22 at the Carlton Building, room 227. Most of us, after we walk out of a meeting, immediately (based on research) forget much of what even went on, much less dates, times and places that will take occur weeks into the future. So start using a calendar in conjunction with the notepad mentioned above, and you will see that you are much more productive and dependable in what you are involved with in your classes and clubs.

> *If you don't think every day is a good day,*
> *just try missing one.*
> —C. Robert

CELL PHONES RULE....UNFORTUNATELY

Do you know anyone without a cell phone? Chances are not many. We all love our phones because of the convenience. Although cell phones have transformed our lives, making communicating with others extremely easy, some people have thrown out common courtesy when that cell phone comes into play. I am convinced people going down on a sinking ship today, if they had a choice of saving their life by swimming with both arms versus drowning by treading water with only one arm so they could hold their cell phone and talk with the other would choose the latter.

Because the problem has become acute, many places have posted signs stating to turn off all cell phones before even approaching. Obviously too many people are continuing or beginning conversations when they are supposed to be conversing with a "live" person. Be mindful of that when using your phone. Do not let the cell phone take precedence over the person standing right in front of you. Let the person calling you leave a message and call that person back or excuse yourself for a moment, answer the phone and tell that person you will call him back. Consider your conversational volume too. Others around you in public places may not want to hear every detail of what you are saying to your phone friend. Exercise common sense and courtesy when using your cell.

> *The function of a leader is to produce more leaders, not more followers.*
> —**Ralph Nader**

CULTIVATE PUNCTUALITY

As with other basic manners, punctuality seems to be less important to some people nowadays. Even if you are from another culture which does not consider punctuality as a big deal, the prevailing norm in this country is still to be on time. If this is a problem for you, then it is a habit that you need to break. When you are supposed to be somewhere at a certain time, you need to be there at that time…period. Think about someone whom you know who is consistently late for everything. Suppose you are the one counting on that person to be on time for some reason? Nobody likes waiting nor do they like being made late because of another's inconsideration.

Being late consistently can hurt your reputation too. A woman whom I worked with was consistently late, even when we had meetings with high-level college officials. These officials were not pleased that she often arrived 30 minutes after a meeting started—always with an excuse. She was eventually fired, and I think the "nail in the coffin" was her habitual tardiness.

Finally, if you are running late, which is unavoidable for all of us at times, then you need to let someone know (in this age of cell phones) that you are running late and when you hope to be there. Do not just leave people hanging.

> *The key to successful leadership*
> *is influence, not authority.*
> —**Unknown**

BUILD YOUR VOCABULARY

Okay, so I was an English major and have been an English instructor so this is "near and dear to my heart." With most people reading less, vocabulary building seems to be dying a slow death. Nevertheless, the ability to articulate well in both speech and writing is a characteristic of many "at the top" and having a larger vocabulary will help you with both areas.

Learning vocabulary is not that difficult. A lot of it is memorization and then using new words. I am not just talking about using "big" words just to impress people; I am talking about learning new words that will give you more than one way to express yourself effectively in speech and writing.

As with any new learning, this will require some effort, but not as much as you might think. Okay, so maybe I was a geek in college; I carried around a notebook full of vocabulary words with me, and when I had a spare minute here or there, I would open it and work on memorizing a few words. I learned hundreds of words that way.

That paid off big time when applying to graduate school. Most exams for graduate school include some type of vocabulary test as part of the verbal section. I know that having a larger vocabulary helped me significantly pull my score up on the Graduate Record Exam. But, in general, having a vocabulary at my disposal that helps me convey my thoughts in words or speech has been a great asset in my profession life, for instance, when I am writing a book.

> *Ability is what you're capable of doing. Motivation determines what you do. Attitude determines how well you do it.*
> —**Lou Holtz**

READ

Ditto above about the English instructor. Ditto, too, the fact that reading seems to have lost a lot of ground in our technologically driven society. But there are a multitude of reasons you should be reading.

Number one: you are going to college and you should be well read. Second: leaders can generally talk about a wide range of topics and much of that knowledge comes from reading. Teddy Roosevelt, one of our most accomplished presidents, and a real "tough guy," was not only a "doer" as a leader, but also a voracious reader and writer. Third: the higher you want to climb in an organization, the more you will be reading, often a lot more. Why? Because you will be keeping up with daily memos, reports, journals, industry trends and whatever else comes across your desk relevant to your position.

Take a break from the internet (unless you are reading websites that are enlightening) and read a book or a magazine, something that will inform you, expand your knowledge and the way you look at the world. Read a wide range of materials, both fiction and non-fiction. Cultivating reading now will pay off later.

I have a cousin and a friend, both who are in their forties and until recently would seemingly only pick up a book if someone put a gun to their heads and threatened to pull the trigger. For different reasons, both began reading on a regular basis. Each has since expressed to me how sorry he was for "wasting" all of those years he could have been reading. If these two guys who thought reading was so blah can rave about how much they enjoy it now, then there has to be something to it!

In regards to leadership, reading, too, can show you examples of how other leaders handled themselves in different situations (some which may be similar to yours), how they led people, how they made decisions, and what did or did not go well. You can pick up new ideas that you can incorporate while developing your own leadership style. Reading will make you a more effective leader, a better-rounded person, a more interesting person, and add to your life's enjoyment (I promise).

> *Leadership is a combination of strategy and character. If you must be without one, be without the strategy.*
> —**Norman Schwarzkopf**

ASK

Need a skill that can be a surprising help to you as you make your way through life, one that if you learn to cultivate could actually change your life in small or large ways. What is that skill? The answer: learn to ask for what you need or want. Sound simplistic? That is because it is. Actually, the simplicity is the beauty behind the power of asking. And asking for something does involve power because you are now focusing on getting something you do not have. Will you always get a yes response? No, not going to happen. However, if you do not ask, you are guaranteed a big, fat zero. On the other hand, many times asking does bring positive results. Think about your own life. Can you think of times you were afraid to ask for something, but went ahead, did it anyway and you got what you asked for? Pretty nifty, huh?

What are some things you can ask for: a return or exchange without a receipt, a person to mentor us, directions (you heard me right guys), a date, help with a club project, money, information, a sale, a raise, help cleaning the apartment from your roommate, whatever is facing you and would benefit you by just asking for what you need.

Why don't we ask for what we want? The main reason is the fear of rejection. We are anticipating the worst. We assume the person we want to ask will say no, get angry, or laugh at us. Any of those could happen but generally will not. And if they do, you will live through it. Think about dating. Although the dating world has changed somewhat, men are still the ones who normally do the asking. How many of us, men, have not asked out a woman because we were so sure she would say no before we even gave it a chance? What were we so afraid of? The answer, of course, is rejection. Nobody likes that feeling.

But, did you have a date with her before you asked? No. If you ask and she says no, do you have a date with her now? No. What has changed? Nothing, except you got a "no," but even rock stars and movie stars ask women out and get no's sometimes. On the other hand, when you have summoned up the courage and gone ahead and asked, haven't you also gotten some yeses? So you got to go out with the hottie after all. Bottom line: if you do not ask, you never know.

Be bold. Most people "out there" are willing to help us in some way if we only ask. But those people are not mind readers and do not know what you are thinking or what you may need unless you make it clear to them. As a professor, I am often surprised that students make mistakes, do not complete assignments or do them incorrectly because they were afraid to ask me for clarification. My job is to help students succeed, not to do every thing I can to fail them, so I am always glad they ask me when they are unsure of something.

Also, learn to ask the right person. Think about a time when you may have a problem with an item you wanted to return to a store and the store policy states you have to have a receipt, you only have 10 days to return it (you are in on day 12), or you did not hold your mouth just right when you bought it.....whatever. The clerk behind the counter immediately says no because of the store policy. So what do you do? Depending on how strongly you feel, you either accept his no or you ask to see the department manager. You then explain the situation to her and she makes a decision, which could or could not be in your favor. But you will never know until you ask and ask the person who has the power to make the call.

Finally, in the leadership realm, realize that you are not expected to be infallible. If you need help in an area, ask for it. We all have strengths and weaknesses. Do not try to fake your way through a situation because your ego will not allow you to ask for help. So in situations you face from now on, "step out onto that tightrope" and practice asking for whatever it is that you need or want; I think you will be surprised at the results.

> *The great leaders are like the best conductors*
> *—they reach beyond the notes to reach*
> *the magic in the players.*
> **—Blaine Lee**

DO YOUR HOMEWORK

I am not just talking about the type of homework for your classes (although that is important!); I am talking about making sure you are informed as a leader especially when facing issues which involve you. For example, if you are in charge of student government and you are asked to join a university–wide committee studying parking problems, then you need to become well versed about parking concerns. Generally, too, you will get materials to read either before or at the initial meeting. If the materials come before the meeting, put some time aside to study them. Do not wait until you are sitting in the meeting to begin educating yourself. If others have done their "homework" and you have not, you may come out looking foolish or feel ignorant (which you will be) versus those who prepared. Also, the material should generate some questions for you.

Do not be shy either about doing some investigating and fact gathering on your own. By this I mean talking to the security office, other students, the administrator on campus in charge of parking, and the finance office to gauge what insights you can gain. You may want to email your peers at other universities to see what they have done to address parking at their institutions. This way you are informed, and you may be able to offer positive solutions to the topic at hand.

Overall, "doing that homework" will pay off. You will know more, you can contribute more, and you will be a valued member of any committee. Not bad.

> *No victor believes in chance.*
> —**Nietzche**

OPEN YOURSELF TO NEW EXPERIENCES

A major purpose of liberal arts education as we know it today evolved through the centuries to expand people's minds and, in turn, broaden their lives. That is one reason you are in college. If you study the lives of great leaders, you will see that many of them had diverse interests, enjoyed a variety of activities and were generally curious by nature. Engaging in all types of experiences enriched their lives.

A few years ago one of my male students approached me before class, asking, "Dr. Paul, you like theatre and all that kind of junk don't you?"

"Yes," I replied, "I do like that kind of 'junk.' Why do you ask?"

"Well, my girlfriend told me the other night that she has tickets to see some play at the performing arts center. She said it is about some guy with a mask, who lives in Paris beneath a church and he kidnaps her, something like that."

"You mean *The Phantom of the Opera*?" I asked.

"Yeah, yeah, that's it. She said she paid a lot of money for tickets, and she wanted to surprise me. But, Dr. Paul, I know I won't like some dumb story with a lot of singing in it."

"I think I can help you. Ask your girlfriend what time I should pick her up and I will go see *The Phantom* for you. I don't want you to suffer."

He laughed. "I am going. I just wondered if you knew anything about the play."

"Yes, I do know something about it. I have seen it twice. Actually Phantom is a musical, not a play per se. People have seen it by the millions, making it one of the most popular musicals ever. Go and watch it with an open mind. Give it a chance."

The next week the student approached me again. "Okay, Dr. Paul, so I went and saw Phantom of the Opera."

"And?" I asked curiously.

"Well, first of all my girlfriend was all dressed up and looked really hot. When we got to the show and it started, I really liked the costumes, the singing, the sets, the whole deal. I was surprised. Now, I wouldn't mind seeing something else."

What a change in attitude he had. Think about your friends who love to try anything. Aren't they more fun, even exciting to hang with because you know they are really living life? Follow their lead. Travel, read a book in a genre you have not read before, bungee jump, take a helicopter ride, skinny dip, eat new kinds of food, visit an art museum, roller blade, attend the symphony, ask her/him out, hear a speaker on a subject you may not know much about, learn a new card game....you get the picture. Trying new experiences will expand your horizons, making you a better-rounded person.

Bottom line: do not automatically assume that you will

not like something new...Let all that money you (or your parents) are paying for a liberal arts education pay off. You will often be pleasantly surprised.

> *There are no impossible dreams; there is just our limited perception of what is possible.*
> —**Unknown**

BE COURTEOUS AND RESPECTFUL TO OTHERS

Courtesy and respect are always trademark indicators of great leaders. Treating people considerately and practicing the Golden Rule always pays big dividends in your relationships with others. Leadership is not ego-driven, at least not in the sense of thinking "I am up here and you are down there so that makes me pretty special." Thinking you are better than others surfaces in your attitude and actions and is noticed quickly. No matter whom you are dealing with, whether a president or janitor, you should treat both equally well.

Practice the simple courtesies in life like saying please and thank you, open doors for others (male and female), be on time, let a car merge in front of you, return phone calls promptly, say good morning to those whom you see in the hallways, say excuse me when needed, keep appointments and perform other courtesies which will enhance the way people perceive you.

President Teddy Roosevelt knew each of the White House staff by name; he spoke to them, learned about each of them personally, and treated each of them with dignity and respect. Many cried openly the day he left. That has not happened with all Presidents. What a great testament to the way he perceived the worth of every individual and how that played out in his life. Practice courtesy; show respect to others and see how that will add to other people's positive perception of you and also add to your own self-esteem.

> *It is not so important who starts the game but who finishes it.*
> —**John Wooden**

PART THREE

OTHER
STUFF

OTHER STUFF

As I mentioned in the preface, this section is a "hodgepodge" of areas that I want to address, ones that are important and can affect you and your lifestyle now as well as in the future. These topics may not seem to relate to character and leadership; however, I believe that you need to look at your life holistically. When you do that, hopefully you'll see that the bulleted headings in this section center on life decisions (most of them) which will be influencing how you live your life more strongly than you might even realize.

As I said, too, some of these areas may be ones that can border on "preachy." However, I hope you will read through them, knowing that we do not know each other, and I am attempting to relay information not only from my experience but from research and suggestions from others who work with students on a daily basis. Whether you agree with what is being said, know that it comes from wanting you to think about these subjects and why they should be of concern to you now.

EXERCISE

When was the last time you exercised? If you cannot remember that far back, or think bringing a slice to a pepperoni pizza to your mouth is a weight lifting exercise, or shifting your positions while lying on the couch is aerobics then you are probably not accomplishing much in the exercise area. Todd Durkin, a personal trainer interviewed in *Vitality Magazine*, says "Studies confirm the more sedentary you are, the more likely you are to lose flexibility, endurance, strength, balance, and coordination, which in turn will affect every aspect of your life." Exercise matters. Here are just a few areas that exercise benefits positively:

Reduces the risk of dying prematurely.

Reduces the risk of dying prematurely from heart disease.

Reduces the risk of developing diabetes.

Reduces the risk of developing high blood pressure.

Helps reduce blood pressure in people who already have high blood pressure.

Reduces the risk of developing colon cancer.

Reduces feelings of depression and anxiety.

Helps control weight.

Helps build and maintain healthy bones, muscles, and joints.

Promotes psychological well-being.

Being out of shape is detrimental at any age; however, most of you are generally in pretty good health simply because of your age. Of course everyone knows that as you age your body starts a slow decline, especially if you are doing nothing in your life to help maintain your body's vitality. Thus, a huge lifestyle choice is whether to make regular exercise part of what you do. Durkin says too, "Incorporating physical activity and exercise into your daily life will help you feel good, look good and thrive in your professional and personal life. If you are physically strong, everything else in your life will fall into place."

Exercising regularly means you enjoy the numerous benefits listed above. What a tremendous difference in the way you will live your life. Why would you not want to do it? For all of us, exercise boils down to self discipline. For those of you who really hate the thought of doing anything physical, the only way will be to force yourself to start. Ease into exercise. Do not begin a workout regimen that would have had Arnold Schwanegger when he was in his prime crying for his mommy. You will quit after the first day. Gradually begin exercising, build momentum, getting you from point A to point B. Exercising now and incorporating it into your lifestyle is another of those decisions which will pay huge dividends so . . . go take a hike . . . literally!

> *No executive has ever suffered because his*
> *subordinates were strong and effective.*
> —Peter Drucker

DIET

First of all, I am not an expert on diet. While researching this area, I was horrified to learn that ice cream and chocolate chip cookies are not considered one of the basic food groups. However, having been a college student and knowing some of the basic eating patterns "of the species," I do know eating proper foods is pretty far down on your "must do" list. Nevertheless, diet, in conjunction with exercise, plays a major role in how you feel and how your body functions. These factors in turn affect your mental and physical health and attitudes. That is why I wanted to address the diet area briefly. According to dietary experts, no ideal diet exists for every person because food needs vary depending on age, sex, body size, physical activity, and other conditions such as pregnancy or illness. Tremendous resources and information are available on eating properly and nutritional health. To confuse matters though, theories galore exist on what proper nutrition and a healthy diet with seemingly a new theory coming out weekly. Fortunately some agreement exists among dieticians who believe certain foods and food groups should be a part of our daily intake. In Appendix 1 I have included Guidelines for Nutrition by the U.S. Food and Drug Administration (see Appendix 1).

Following are dietary guidelines for Americans (listed by the U.S. Department of Health and Human Services):

Eat a variety of foods (pizza with 6 different toppings does not count), including fruits and vegetables.

Maintain ideal weight (easier said than done…based on American food choices)

Avoid too much fat, saturated fat, and cholesterol.

Eat foods with adequate starch and fiber.

Avoid too much sugar (hear that soft drink junkies?).

Avoid too much sodium.

If you drink alcohol, do so in moderation.

Diet is an area that will affect you mentally and physically. Being a college student means a lot of fast food and irregular meals. Plus, the eating habits you cultivate now can affect your body for years to come. Although this area may not seem important to many now, at least think about your body as a well-oiled machine that needs to be maintained properly to continue to function well.

> *One of the tests of leadership is*
> *the ability to recognize a problem before*
> *it becomes an emergency.*
> —**Arnold Glasgow**

HIT THE SACK

Some of you need to go to bed more and stay longer.....alone....
and get some sleep. The whole realm of sleep deprivation and
all of the subsequent negative consequences have been detailed
for years in many scholarly publications. Cutting back on sleep
is an extremely common response to the time pressures of
modern industrial societies. The average night's sleep decreased
from about nine hours in 1910 to about 7.5 hours in 1975, a
trend that continues (*Science Daily*, 1999). In our fast-paced
society with everyone scurrying around, people are sleeping less
hours per night. Many college students are no exception. Some
of you work jobs with a lot of hours, take a full-time course
load, spend time studying (some spend serious time) and try
to continue to "party down" whenever you can. Sleep is placed
on the "back burner" and not given the importance it should
receive. Unfortunately, the loser in the whole frenetic pace is
you.

Also, many people are aware that alcohol-related car accidents are prevalent and claim thousands of lives each year, but did you know that the National Highway Traffic Safety Administration (NHTSA) estimates conservatively that each year drowsy driving is responsible for at least 100,000 automobile crashes, 71,000 injuries, and 1,550 fatalities.

That's driving. What happens in your normal routine when you don't get the sleep you need? The bottom line is the less sleep you get the less effective and alert you are as a human being. Prolonged sleep deprivation leads to increased fatigue, poor attention and motivation spans, memory lapses, poor judgment and difficulty in dealing with others. Thus, you are immediately exhibiting characteristics of three of the seven dwarfs: Sleepy, Grumpy and Dopey. Wouldn't that explain why you are not yourself when you are not getting enough sleep?

Weekends in college are hectic and fun; they are supposed to be. Sleeping is not a big consideration when you are out "walking on the wild side." However, know that your body craves that sleep it is missing and at least try to grab some short naps on the weekends and do whatever you can during the week (go to bed earlier) to make-up for some of that lost sleep. Your body and mind will both appreciate that extra sleep and the rejuvenated you will be an even more sparkling, arresting personality than you are now—if that's possible!

> *Quit making excuses and go after*
> *what YOU want in life.*
>
> —Earl Paul

MARTYRDOM FOR SOME
STUDENT LEADERS

One observation I have about some campus leaders is they are too busy, taking on too many commitments, "juggling too many balls in the air." Although wanting to be involved in seemingly everything is commendable, what you are doing is stressing yourself out, not doing as well with the responsibilities you have assumed, and basically running around like a "wild man or woman" hoping to just keep up. *You do not have to volunteer nor be involved or take a leadership role in everything.* Yes, it may seem as if you do not volunteer to do it, it will not get done, but, if that is true, too bad. Quit overextending yourself and concentrate on doing a few things well and not driving yourself crazy.

One student at our college assumed a leadership role in numerous organizations. She proudly signed her emails with her various club titles: President of this, VP of that, and Secretary-Elect. A lot of impressive titles, but guess what? No one could depend on "superwoman" to attend meetings or follow through on responsibilities she had pledged to handle. She was so wrapped up in her titles and being important that she was spreading herself too thin and doing nothing well. In her daily conversations, she was "all about" how tired and stressed she was, there were not enough hours in the day, blah, blah, blah ... well, duh. If you are one of these people, relax, lessen your commitments and concentrate on being involved in a few activities and devoting quality time to them. Martyrdom does not really mean a lot when you are the one sacrificing yourself.

> *Treat people as if they were what they ought to be and you help them to become what they are capable of being.*
> —Johann Van Goethe

VOTE

Although alluding to patriotism and flag waving seems to upset many today, the truth is thousands of American military men and women have died throughout our country's history in numerous wars to defend the democratic way of life that we enjoy. Underlying the whole democratic structure is the privilege that we have to vote for people we want to see put in or out of office. All countries in the world have not had nor do they have this right today. Do not take this privilege lightly. Learn the issues and the candidates' stances, then exercise your voting rights sanctioned by our Constitution.

According to the Center for Information and Research, the number of 18-24 year old American citizens in 2004 eligible to vote was 24.9 million. Those who voted: 11.7 million (47%). This number was actually up 11 percentage points from the 2000 election. Just for a comparison, the number of eligible voters over 25: 172.1 million and 114.1 million (66%) voted. So the 18-25 year old group is lagging behind the older group, but participation, at least in the last election, was on the upswing. Good news.

Another observation on voting. Should you always vote based on your party affiliation? Hopefully not. Too many people are sheep-like, voting based solely on which party they registered with. Blue states. Red states. Voting nationwide is split "right down the middle." Although this two party system has been traditional throughout history, my observation is the system browbeats people into being for one or the other parties and not leaving much room for disagreement. My charge to you is use your brain and your best judgment and vote based on what the issues are and what the person stands for. You will have to stay informed and become open-minded, but that should be a vital part of your educational process.

> *Only those who will risk going too far can*
> *possibly find out how far one can go.*
> —T. S. Eliot

GET YOUR DEGREE

Stay in college. Get the diploma. Education does matter. Hopefully you have seen some of the articles and statistics about how much more money a college graduate makes than a high school graduate or how much more a high school graduate makes versus no high school diploma. True. Professional occupations (white collar) for the most part require a four year college degree. Ironically, what the degree is in may not make a bit of difference to some employers; they just want you to have the degree. Not having that diploma will automatically exclude you from any consideration at many companies. If you do not believe me, start calling around and ask what minimum requirements are for hiring.

Plus, once you have dropped out of college, coming back at a later period may be much more difficult than you imagined. Even if you do not see the relevance of having a degree now or you want to make a statement by dropping out, you will most likely regret that decision some day.

And ladies I am not trying to be chauvinistic in this area, but I am telling you that I have encountered a number of middle-aged women in my classes over the years who found Mr. Right, who later turned out to be Mr. Wrong. The same guy who promised to love them forever, traded the wife in for the younger secretary, and he was gone. Unfortunately, most of these "suddenly single" women had dropped out of college to start a family, so they had no degree and a shortage of work experience. You will never regret getting that degree, even if you marry Mr. Right before finishing college. Get the degree now while you can, while you are younger and not worrying about the complicated issues you will have if you are trying to work, raise kids, and go to college at night. Someday if you are looking, you may have to "brush up" on some areas or convince a hiring person that you are a viable candidate even though you have been at home for many years, but the hurdle of not having a college degree will not be staring you in the face.

> *To become fully alive a person must have goals and aims that transcend himself.*
> —**Herbert Otto**

PICKING A MAJOR

If you are reading this book and not sure what you want to do as far as a major, do not feel like the Lone Ranger (do you know who that is?). Many students like you are not exactly sure what the heck they want to major in and the panicky feelings associated with that are all too real. Loosen up. If you are serious about finding a major, I guarantee you that there is not a university, four year private college, or community college in existence without a career resource center anxiously awaiting students like you to come see them. This is what these people do…for free. They help students through testing, counseling, research, internships, site visits, and whatever other means they have to match you with a relevant field.

Another great resource they can "hook you up with" is interest tests. I have had some experience with these interest inventories in my work and doctoral program and can tell you that these tests can give you excellent insights into fields which you would truly enjoy. Popular interest tests are highly valid and reliable (testing jargon for "you can depend on the results"). The final exciting feature is the tests will be freebies or have a minimal charge associated with them. Not true out in the real world. So if you are getting schizophrenic about what to major in, go invest some time at your career center. You might be surprised about some of the things you learn about yourself as well as getting some terrific advice to help you out.

Finally, an excellent book exists, written especially for college students on the whole realm of making your college experience more successful and finding a major and a "cool" job. The book, *Major in Success* by Patrick Combs, is a must read for all college students. The insights are invaluable for your college years and career afterwards.

> *The best job goes to the person who can get it done without passing the buck or coming back with excuses.*
> —Napoleon Hill

CREDIT CARDAHOLICS

Show me the money! At least show me the plastic if I cannot see the money. Credit cards for many, including college students, are symbols of money they do not have but are spending anyway with reckless abandon. Debt in this country has spiraled out of control. According to a report by the television show FRONTLINE® and the *New York Times,* more than 641 million credit cards are in circulation, accounting for an estimated $1.5 trillion of consumer spending. The estimated present debt level nationwide is 600 *billion* dollars. That is a hell of a big number in anybody's eyes. The average undergraduate has $2,200 in credit card debt, according to Nellie Mae, the nation's largest maker of student loans. That figure jumps to $5,800 for graduate students.

People are not climbing out of that debt very quickly. One sobering example: by sticking to minimum payments, the average student would take more than 12 years and $1,115 in interest to pay off a $1,000 bill on a card with an 18 percent annual rate. Yikes! Unfortunately, many college students are in credit card debt, so much so that some drop out because their debt levels become unmanageable. For a few, using credit cards is just as addicting as gambling, alcohol or drugs. Two other unhappy by-products of debt include diverting money from the repayment of student loans or later trying unsuccessfully to obtain other credit (a mortgage for instance).

At my college, we have had credit card companies "sneak" on campus, set up a table, and give away t-shirts to any student who will open an account. Students swarm their tables like bees to honey, happily filling out applications. Just like cigarette manufacturers, these folks are hoping to get you hooked, the younger the better. Unfortunately, if the situation is not bad enough, some companies and banks are actually now doing all that they can to reap even more profits from credit cards. The trap many do not see is hidden in the fine print of the agreements people sign to get the cards. Call the 800 number on your card and ask someone to explain the terms to you if you have any questions.

Following are some steps that can help you successfully manage your credit cards.

Certainly the best strategy is to pay off your credit card monthly. But if you get behind, always pay the minimum amount owed (preferably more). Remember, however, paying off the minimum each month does little towards paying off the principle.

A way that credit card companies make huge profits is by assessing fees if the bill is not paid on time. To "trip up" their own customers, they are resorting to pulling stunts like shortening the time card holders have to pay off their balances. Late payments can also be more expensive because you will incur penalties, extra fees, or additional finance charges. Thus, make sure you know exactly what date a payment is due and get that payment in a couple of days ahead of time. Even being late a few hours can cost you big time.

Another great tactic for you to use is to limit your card's spending limit, even if the bank would happily approve much more, to a relatively small amount, say a few hundred dollars at the most. That way you know your balance will not get out of hand and it will be easier to pay off.

Anytime you make a credit card payment, assuming you have a checkbook, subtract the amount you just charged from your checkbook balance, thus insuring the money is there at the end of the month when you are to pay your bill.

If you ever change your mailing address, make sure your credit card company knows immediately so the bill they send to you will not be forwarded by the U.S. mail, tacking on days to the delivery time, making your payment late, and bringing the accompanying "bad news."

Obviously credit cards are an integral part of our society; with all of the money involved and the popularity of the cards, that fact will not change. Your goal should be to learn to use credit cards wisely and frugally. If you are one of those people who cannot handle a credit card because your eyes glaze over and your senses leave you, then do not get one or cut yours up until you can control yourself. Otherwise, when you get out of college, the mound of debt you accrue could be an albatross hanging around your neck, one that will be hanging there for years.

> *It's okay to fail. If you're not failing,*
> *you're not growing.*
> —H. Stanley Judd

PEER PRESSURE

Young adults (as do a fair amount of older adults) love to fit in with the crowd. If they do not, they feel they have failed in some respect. That feeling of wanting to belong at almost any cost is called peer pressure, a very real phenomenon. We have all dealt with it. Being concerned about what your friends would think or say about what you are doing, wearing, saying, planning, and who you are dating become an obsession for some. The paradox of peer pressure is that you are so far into it that you don't even know you're there. That is why you do much of what you do, why we all do so much of what we do when we are younger. Again, normal. An interesting aspect of aging is looking back on your life and seeing how concerned you were with about what everyone thought of you. Part of maturation, however, should be slowly separating yourself from the crowd, your parents, your friends, your siblings and living your own life based much less on peer pressure and other's influence and more on what you want to do. Realize that you cannot and should not live your life based on what you think everyone else is going to think of you.

I knew a guy, "John" who, when in college, joined some buddies (who had been drinking) and headed out in the country with them to see how fast a new car could go on some back roads. He said he had a "bad feeling" about going, knowing his pals had downed a few beers, but they kept bugging him. So he went. Now he spends his life in a wheelchair as a paraplegic because his buddy lost control of the car and rammed into a tree. The buddy later died. What a price John pays now for ignoring his "little voice," for taking a ride with friends who had been drinking just so he could be one of the guys.

Early adult years are a time of wanting to be a part of the crowd and experimentation, no doubt about it. Most of us have participated in some wilder stuff, sometimes dumb stuff because we are younger and that is part of the thrill of the age. But a line has to be drawn sometimes and the choice of drawing that line is yours. Thus, if you are getting pressured to do something that you do not want to do; do not do it! Leave wherever you are if you have to. Take the jibes. Having the courage to say no is much more impressive, requiring much more character than "just going along because everyone else is doing it," whatever "it" is. If you are not comfortable with a situation, do not follow the crowd, especially if harm could come to you in some way.

> *No man will make a great leader who*
> *wants to do it all himself or to get*
> *all the credit for doing it.*
> **—Andrew Carnegie**

SAVE SOME BUCKS

Save money, plan for retirement? Are you kidding? At your age, that is the last thing you are worrying about. You are in college, so for most of you that means that saving money is laughable because every cent you make is already spoken for, and you are already wondering how you are going to pay for books and tuition next semester, much less worry about putting some money aside. Okay, so saving money may not be much of an option now, but being aware as soon as you can that beginning a saving's plan will have to be a priority in your lifetime. Social Security is in trouble and business pensions are going away so more and more Americans are going to have to start saving additional money for longer periods if they want a retirement free from anxiety and worry over how to make ends meet.

A main reason many Americans do not do well financially in the long run is not because they do not make a nice income, it is because they do not know how to manage their earnings. As a college graduate someday, chances are you will be one of those people who at least makes the median income. However, if you are like most Americans today, long range planning and financial management are not high priorities. That is evident when looking at the dire conditions many are facing, whether in credit card debt (as already discussed), the saving's rate of the average American (about 1% today) or the spend, spend mentality that many of us possess in a materialistic society that certainly encourages that mentality.

When looking at the fact that about half of Americans retire (now) in financial trouble, even with social security presently being paid to millions, how bad is that going to be 40 years from now, when you are retiring, if the social security system is scaled back tremendously or insolvent. Some financial experts today are telling people to plan for retirement, not figuring in social security because it may not be there. And that is a concern because so many Americans today are dependent on Social Security. Presently, about 25% of all retirees get all their income from Social Security, and for two-thirds it is their primary source of income. And not only is Social Security in trouble, but other pension plans are being dissolved or no longer offered. Companies are no longer willing to pay the millions into retirement funds. For retirees today, 22% get a pension from a past private-sector employer, and 13% from a past public-sector employer. That leaves 65% of today's retirees who are on their own. That percentage will be higher for you, as even fewer private sector companies will continue having a pension annuity.

If you read any book on saving and investing, however, each stresses the importance of saving and investing money, the sooner the better. These books emphasize the miracle of compounding interest over long periods of time and how that can insure that you can have a large nest egg based on saving over many years. Even a small amount each week or month, if left alone, can become a large number if allowed to accumulate for 30 or so years. Financial experts also talk about the concept of paying yourself first (taking money out of your paycheck automatically and investing it) and how important that concept is for accumulating money.

I am not going into strategies and plans, what works and does not work according to the experts. I have included a couple of basic books in the appendix that covers what you can start doing now to make sure you can retire comfortably. My main point is that based on the economy, the shakiness of Social Security, and the disappearance of pension plans, know that you are going to be more responsible for your own retirement. Believe me, I understand that retirement seems light years away, but I just want this section to at least make you start thinking NOW that this is an area you will have to address for your long-term well being.

> *All greatness is achieved while performing outside your own comfort zone.*
> —A. Arnold

TATTOO MANIA

First of all, I am not just an "older person" who is against tattoos. I know they are "what is hot" today, and many are attractive. My main point centers on asking you to think before permanently inking yourself — where you place the tattoos and how much of your body they will cover. The permanent tattoo you add to your body at 18 may not be as attractive to you as you age. Believe it or not, many of you will get a little more conservative as you get older, and the tattoo that extends the length of your leg or arm or extends around the back of your neck may not seem quite as appealing as it was while you were in college.

Plus, there are those people in the world who do not like tattoos and who are in hiring positions. If you go into a job interview with tattoos that are immediately noticeable, that could be a deciding factor. Of course that person with hiring power would not tell you that for fear of a law suit, but it will happen with some.

As you know, too, tattoos are expensive to put on and even more expensive to get off. I have read that 25% of people who have gotten tattoos are now trying to get them "lasered off." Someday you may be one of them. I overheard some female students talking recently, and one said she wished she had not gotten such a large tattoo on her back. If she had to do it over, she would have gotten one much smaller. So before you go "all out," think about the possibility that you may someday want to have the tattoo removed or not be as visible. Let that be your guide of how large you want it and where you want it.

> *Individual commitment to a group effort—that's what makes a team work.*
>
> —Vince Lombardi

SPARE TIME

Most of us are gifted in life with a certain amount of spare time, depending on what stage of life we are in. Generally, though, most college students have time they can call their own. What we choose to do with that spare time while in college, and when you leave college, can produce drastically different results for different people. The average American watches an average of six hours a day per week of television. Yikes! Just think of the investment of time that the person is losing forever "vegging out" on the couch staring at TV.

My challenge to you is to take 25% of the time you are wasting (yes, wasting), let's say 5 hours per week, and start putting those five hours towards goals in whatever areas you choose. You will be amazed at how much you can accomplish in five hours of concentrated effort. And you are only using hours you were not doing anything with anyway — how cool is that? I read a goal setting book that made this point, examined my life, and realized I could devote more time to more constructive pursuits (like writing this book). Use those five hours and exercise more, concentrate on your hobbies, STUDY, read about leadership or people who have been great leaders, spend quality time with other people, learn a new language, whatever can improve your life. Devoting five hours a week to anything for an extended period can make you an expert or proficient in just about any area. So become more productive and apply that spare time to constructive interests.

The nose of a bulldog is slanted back, so that he can still breathe without ever letting go.
—**Winston Churchill**

SARCASM

Although sarcasm can be funny to many people who like it, numerous people do not get it or do not appreciate it, especially if it is at their expense. And whatever you do in a leadership role, do not use sarcasm in public with anyone whom you are leading. Public contempt is the worst.

We had a female vice-president of SGA who loved to ridicule others in meetings if they came up with an idea that she did not like. She would literally say how stupid she thought their ideas were. I talked to her two or three times about how criticizing others in public could really be "the pits" for them. She finally "got it" for the meetings; however, she continued to hammer others and their ideas when interacting outside of the meeting setting. Needless to say, by the end of the year, she was not a popular leader or person.

Another reason to be careful is many people do not forget sarcastic or cutting remarks aimed at them (ever), and they may be hoping to "get even with you" someday. So when you have a choice of whether to make that brilliant comment or not (and you know no one is holding a gun to your head to make it), the smart move is to keep your mouth shut. Save it for your friends if they can take it, but my advice as a recovering "Sarcastic Mouth," is cut out as much of it as you can with everyone.

> *The only things in life you ever regret are the chances you didn't take and to hell with the consequences!*
> **—Unknown**

SMOKING

Okay, here is one topic many of you do not want to hear about and some will skip over. But for those who are willing to read on, I hope you will do so with an open mind. I am devoting more space to this topic because of the significant impact smoking can have in numerous areas of your life.

First of all, the reason that you smoke is peer pressure. That is it. Smoking is the ultimate example of people wanting to "fit in," so they do what so many others are doing so they can be "cool" too. You did not start smoking because everyone had been telling you how good smoking is in every respect, how much smoking would improve your looks or your health. You did not start because when you took that first drag of a cigarette, your body thrilled to the intake of smoke into healthy lungs. I bet, too, your parents did not march you proudly into a convenience store at 14 and say "Honey, you are mommy's and daddy's little girl (or boy), we are so proud of you, we think it is time you move on to the next level of maturity, so we want to have the honor of buying you your first pack of cigarettes."

Everyone, including the tobacco companies, knows that smoking, especially prolonged smoking, has dire health consequences for many people. Statistics galore substantiate that fact. And do the tobacco companies have your best interest at heart or are they more concerned with making money? Interestingly enough, as I write this section, a big news story is breaking, centering on cigarette makers being caught adding more nicotine to their cigarettes —- all brands. And guess what brands are being targeted - those most popular with young adults (and children). If the companies did not want you to become addicted, would they being adding more nicotine to cigarettes? Doesn't seem to follow, does it? Or does the logic follow that these companies know that addicted teens turn into a "cash cow" for life.

Some decisions that you make now *can* affect you the rest of your life; choosing to smoke is one of those decisions. When you are younger, you feel invincible. That is part of being younger. The idea of getting old, seriously ill or dying is not really on the radar screen for most average, fairly healthy young adults. And for most of you, statistics (again) are on your side.

However, the long term effects are the bad news. I remember my mother was upset about my sister smoking because she started so young (about 14), but my mother could not say much because she smoked. [Eventually my mother died of lung cancer]. My sister smoked into her early forties and was hooked, big time. And she lamented to me one day that she would love to stop smoking, but she just could not; there was no way. About a year later, a lump appeared in her left breast, one that turned out to be malignant. To hopefully stop the cancer, she had a mastectomy. Funny thing, the day the doctor explained to her that she had breast cancer, she stopped smoking ... cold turkey. With death staring you in the face, motivation to live becomes a high priority.

No doubt about it, though, the choice you have made to smoke will have repercussions, sometimes serious ones, for you eventually. Not everyone who smokes develops cancer, and, yes, for those of you who are thinking I could also be killed in a car accident (whatever) and I still drive, so why not smoke?

Although the logic seems reasonable, it is not. For any addict, smoking will have numerous negative health issues associated with it throughout your lifetime. One question: if you could see into the future and know that smoking would shorten your life or cause you to have a disease(s) that could have been prevented had you not smoked, what would you do? You may not believe me now, but those of you who have made the decision to not smoke or to quit will look back someday at that decision as being one of your wisest. (By the way, thanks for reading this section to the end).

Leadership is action, not position.
—Donald H. McGannon

LITTERING

How lame can I be, talking about litter? But count this as one of those little issues that reflects on you and your character. If you do not know it, our population is spiraling out of control world-wide. That means more and more people are crowding in, living together. With billions of people sharing the planet, the "little things" do count. I see students throwing down soft drink cups as they walk around campus, leaving bottles on the grass when they are finished, emptying their car ashtrays in the parking lot and throwing fast food bags out of car windows as they are heading home.

Is this really no big deal? To me, littering reflects a type of arrogance and self centeredness, assuming that leaving trash lying around or tossing it out for someone else to pick up is okay. Trashing where you live, where we all live, should be a concern. I have been in third world countries where litter is everywhere and trash is not collected — not a pretty sight.

Again, your character reflects many of the daily choices you make. If you are a litterer, you are exhibiting a callous attitude. Take the step of being conscious of your surroundings and lay off tossing trash anywhere and everywhere. Practice environmental manners. If you are one of the more educated people on the planet and you cannot control "trashing the planet," who will?

Setting goals is the first step in turning
the invisible into the visible.
—Anthony Robbins

TANNING

Come on, how can tanning and hitting the beach be a big deal? For many of you who have more melanin (the pigment that helps protect your skin), you may have less concern, although you are not automatically immune from the sun's rays. I am writing especially to those who are fair skinned, light haired and light eyed, who could be in "a heap" of trouble, maybe not today, but as the years pass and the sun damages surfaces. More and more people seem to be "getting it" as far as worshipping the sun for hours on end. But some are still stubborn, believing sun exposure is no big deal. With global warming and less ozone, the sun's rays are stronger; believe the scientists. And the big "C" is what you will be looking forward to. Skin cancer is a cumulative disease. Most of you will not see the damage that has been done until many years have passed. But once the skin cancers begin popping out, they are tenacious.

I have had nine skin cancers operations, including having my left ear re-built and none of the operations was fun. But I spent countless hours on the beaches of Florida, played tennis, bicycled thousands of miles, swam, worked summers out of doors, lathered on the baby oil and basically fried, peeled and tanned my way through life. Being blonde-haired, fair skinned and blue eyed did not help. Plus, we were not as aware of the harm that prolonged sun exposure could do then like we are now.

I am not saying forget the sun. But, heed the warnings of dermatologists who are trying very hard to make everyone understand that too much sun is harmful. And avoid tanning beds and salons like you are being chased by the Ebola virus; the rays you catch in tanning salons are just as deadly as lying directly in the sun. The solution: check out fake tans. No longer do you have to look like an orange skinned freak; the products now are much better and tans look real. Plus, you are avoiding the skin damage (do you really want to look all wrinkly at an earlier age?). So look bronzed and tanned, just use the fake sun out of a bottle versus the real sun or tanning salons. This is an appropriate place for one of those "some day you will be glad you did" statements.

Aim for the highest.
—**Andrew Carnegie**

LAST QUICK TIP

When you finish college and you are heading out into the working world, especially if you are looking for a job, you need to get a second email address versus the one you may be using now. You can no longer be "Studman@," "Hotbabe4u@," "Thedog@," whatever you might be using in your present life when sending emails, especially if the emails are going to prospective employers. Choose a blander name for emails going to the public; save the "rad" one for your friends.

> *This one step - choosing a goal and sticking to it - changes everything.*
> **—Scott Reed**

FINAL THOUGHTS

Remember, when talking about character, a person who says no to something that many other people are doing exhibits more strength of character than those who "cave" and do what everyone else is doing just to fit in. I hope you will be one of those "non-cavers." Following like a sheep is not leadership nor is character required. Resiliency of character means being consistent and continuing to follow your conscience or inner compass when others are pressuring you to conform to what they are thinking or doing.

Fair warning, though, a person with character has a more difficult life in many respects than those people who choose to go along with the crowd. To stand up for an issue you believe in when many others do not, to say no when most other people are saying yes, and to choose a path that is less traveled because of the difficulties that will accompany it are all choices some prior leaders have chosen and have paid the price by attracting ridicule and misunderstanding.

Realize that you can start choosing *now* what you want to do with your life. And choosing is what you will do because so much of our lives involve making choices. Listen to that inner voice that guides you. Learn to ask yourself daily how you can become a better person. Or notice successful people and ask yourself what qualities you see that you would like to develop. Or what is a new habit or skill that I need to work on to help me in life? When you do make the conscious choice to make some changes or develop some new habits, do not expect it to happen all at once. Learning anything or changing behavior is not going to happen overnight. You will make some progress, then go back a couple of steps, and then go forward. That is the way we all learn. Just make sure and commend yourself for this type of self improvement; fewer people than you realize are consciously doing it.

Accept that leadership development is a lifelong commitment. As with any learned skill, the more you learn about it and the more you practice and innovate, the better off you will be. Approach leading others as a challenge, one that will test you and force you to grow. Know you will never do everything right in the leadership realm as with all areas of life, but that investing in bettering yourself will be the best choice that you can ever make.

Strive to be different, at least in character, to be a person who has integrity, who has regard for him/herself and others, who attempts to live his life as a positive example. And that is difficult nowadays with so many in our society advocating for and defending almost any behavior and ridiculing those with strong moral fiber. Force of character is an incredible asset as well as a powerful way to live. Rights and wrongs do exist, no matter what liberal thinkers say, no matter what our media says, no matter how so many other famous and ordinary people live their lives today.

Look for role models; search for people in books, in history, or in literature who have chosen to live exemplary lives. Moral leaders conduct that search, finding people to emulate. Be different. Set your personal standards high. Do not let others dictate what they think is best for you. You do have one life on this earth and although some in our society believe in reincarnation, even they do not believe that you (or anyone) will come back as the same person. So you have one shot. If you start planning now how you want to live your life, you will not have to look back when you are much older and think about all of those things that should have been—the places you could have gone, the people you could have treated better, the leader you could have been, the volunteer work you could have done, or the positive influence you could have had on others.

Focus on getting better in those areas where you are developing and discovering your individual strengths and talents. What gets your juices flowing? What do you do the best, what comes easy to you, what do you like to do? Do you paint well, write well, think creatively, solve equations that stump the rest of us, encourage others, sell steaks to vegetarians because your selling skills are that good, write computer programs that kick butt, or sing like a songbird. These are gifts people! I concentrate on teaching, speaking, writing, and administrating because that is where I shine We all have unique gifts. Use them, exploit them, enjoy them. If you do, you will be much happier in life because you are drawing from those areas of strength deep inside of you that make you special. I am not advocating ignoring your weaknesses; address them and become competent in areas that are not as strong for you, but concentrate on nurturing your strengths.

Emphasizing character development affords you the base you will need to draw from as you take on more leadership tasks and guide more people. Leadership also is an active process and requires learning skills, so start practicing and learning now while you are younger. If you do, as you age, you hone those skills,

Work hard, play hard, love hard, stand up for what you believe in, help others, do not make excuses, give to worthy causes, get involved in worthy causes, tell the truth, take up for those who work for you, do not follow the crowd every time, exercise, worship your God if that is part of your life, persist when others would quit, be someone who keeps her word, vote, listen to others when they speak, pick out what you want to do in life and go after it with gusto, do not be rude with your cell phone, lead by example, follow when you need to follow, cry when you need to cry, go the "extra mile" without being asked, read, do not cheat others, be considerate of others, eat some healthy food along with the junk, do not cheat yourself, understand that leading is an honor and should be seen that way, make the best choices you can and then go on, keep a positive attitude, treat animals with kindness, practice the Golden Rule, genuinely compliment someone everyday, write thank you notes, help when you do not have to, be open to others' viewpoints, and do practice and embody the numerous other acts and traits that will make you a person of character and a stronger leader.

Begin a transformational process now to make the character qualities defined in the first section of this book part of your make-up. Character *does* matter. Work on building yours. Remember, too, that leadership is learned. Study, observe and practice what produces an effective leader. If you do, you will stand out and become someone who leads others well. I wish you all the best in your journey.

APPENDIX I

BASIC NUTRITIONAL GUIDELINES

Basic nutritional guidelines which generally apply to healthy individuals over the age of two years would be:

Daily, drink 64 to 80 ounces of water/water based beverages:

Water

Fruit Juices

Vegetable Juices

Milk

Make grains a staple: six to eleven servings per day of:

Breads

Cereals

Rice

Pasta

[The American Dietetic Association and the USDA (U.S. Dept of Agriculture) recommend that a minimum of three of these servings come from whole grains.]

[Note: Eleven total servings applies to those who are both

big and active, thus require 2,800 calories each day; whereas six servings would be appropriate for small, inactive individuals who consume just 1,600 calories per day.]

Include two to four servings of fruit each day.

Include three to five servings of vegetables each day.

Include two to three servings per day of Dairy products.

Milk

Cheese

Yogurt

Include two to three servings per day of high-protein foods:

Lean Meat

Poultry

Fish

Cooked Dry Beans

Eggs

Nuts

Include 20 to 30 grams of Fiber each day. High fiber foods include:

Fruits

Vegetables

Whole-Grain Products

Cooked Dry Beans

Limit consumption of salt, sweets and alcohol. To help limit sugar and salt, buy Fewer Pre-Prepared Foods or Look for Low-Sodium Products.

Eat Fresh Fruit for Dessert.

Try salt substitute and artificial sugar.

Limit dietary intake of saturated fat and cholesterol. To help decrease dietary fat:

When eating meat, choose lean meat and trim the fat; trim the skin from poultry.

Broil, poach, steam and bake foods instead of frying.

When baking, substitute fruit puree for some or all of the butter or oil in recipes.

Choose low-fat or no-fat dairy products.

Limit use of high-fat condiments such as mayonnaise, salad dressing, butter, and margarine.

Instead of a rich dessert try fruit.

Avoid fast-food restaurants.

Choose "heart-healthy" alternatives when eating out.

Try fat substitutes.

Eating a wide variety of foods from all food groups is the best way to help ensure adequate intake of essential vitamins and minerals.

For individuals who cannot or do not consume an adequate variety of foods, however, a multi-vitamin/multi-mineral supplement may be beneficial.

SUGGESTED READINGS

Cannon, J. & Cannon, J. (2003). *Leadership Lessons of the Navy Seals*. The McGraw- Hill Companies.

Carlson, R. (1997). *Don't Sweat The Small Stuff . . . and it's all small stuff*. Hyperion: New York.

Carnegie, D. (1981 Revised Edition). *How To Win Friends & Influence People*. Simon & Schuster, Inc.: New York.

Combs, P. (2003). *Major in Success*. Berkeley: Ten Speed Press.

Cottrell, D. & Harvey, E. (2004). *Leadership Courage*. Dallas: The Walk The Talk Company.

Covey, S. (2004). *The 7 Habits of Highly Effective People: Restoring the Character Ethic*. New York: Free Press.

Giuliani, R. (2002). *Leadership*. New York: Hyperion.

Kouzes, J. & Posner, B. (1995). *The Leadership Challenge*. San Francisco: Jossey-Bass Publishers.

Maxwell, J. (1999). *The 21 Indispensable Qualities Of A Leader*. Nashville: Thomas Nelson, Inc.

SUGGESTED READINGS

Maxwell, J. (1998). *The 21 Irrefutable Laws Of Leadership.* Nashville: Thomas Nelson, Inc.

Schwartz, D. (1987). *The Magic of Thinking Big.* New York: Simon & Schuster, Inc.

Winget, L. (Ed.). (1996). *Only The Best on Leadership.* Tulsa: Win Publications.

Readings on Wealth Building/Savings

Bach, D. (2004). *The Automatic Millionaire: A Powerful One-Step Plan to Live and Finish Rich.* New York: Broadway Books.

Chilton, D. (1995). *The Wealthy Barber: Everyone's Commonsense Guide to Becoming Financially Independent.* Prima Publishing.

WEBSITES ON LEADERSHIP

www.leadershipsociety.com

www.ptk.org

www.apca.com

www.asgaonline.com

www.gammabetaphi.org

www.ncssleadership.com

www.paperclipcommunications.com

www.changezone.co.uk/weblinks/leadwebs.html

www.circlek.org/circlek/

http://www.12manage.com/i_l.html

http://psychology.about.com/od/leadership/p/leadtheories.htm

SUGGESTED READINGS

WEBSITES ON CHARACTER

http://education.csufresno.edu/bonnercenter/character_edu
cation_links.html

http://www.school-for-champions.com/character/resources.htm

http://cte.jhu.edu/techacademy/web/2000/kochan/
charactertraits.html

ORDERING AND CONTACT INFORMATION

To order copies of *So You Want to be a Leader?* go to Dr. Paul's website www.drearlpaul.com

Also if you're looking for a informative, thought provoking speaker, Dr. Paul is available to come to your campus. If you are the student who initially contacts him and gets him booked at your campus, you will be paid a "finder's fee" of $100.

To contact him with questions or comments, you can email him at info@drearlpaul.com